REDEFINING
FAIR

How to Plan, Assess, and Grade for Excellence in Mixed-Ability Classrooms

DAMIAN COOPER

Solution Tree | Press

a division of
Solution Tree

555 North Morton Street
Bloomington, IN 47404

800.733.6786 (toll free) / 812.336.7700
FAX: 812.336.7790

email: info@solution-tree.com
solution-tree.com

Printed in the United States of America

19   18   17   16   15   6   7   8   9   10

Library of Congress Cataloging-in-Publication Data

Cooper, Damian.
    Redefining fair : how to plan, assess, and grade for excellence in mixed-ability classrooms / Damian Cooper.
        p. cm.
    ISBN 978-1-935542-14-8 (perfect bound) -- ISBN 978-1-935542-15-5 (library edition) 1. Mixed ability grouping in education--United States. 2. Learning ability. 3. Classroom management--United States. I. Title.
    LB3061.3.C66 2011
    371.2'520973--dc23
                        2011018662

Solution Tree
Jeffrey C. Jones, CEO & President

Solution Tree Press
President: Douglas M. Rife
Publisher: Robert D. Clouse
Vice President of Production: Gretchen Knapp
Managing Production Editor: Caroline Wise
Senior Production Editor: Edward Levy
Proofreader: Elisabeth Abrams
Text and Cover Designer: Orlando Angel

ACKNOWLEDGMENTS

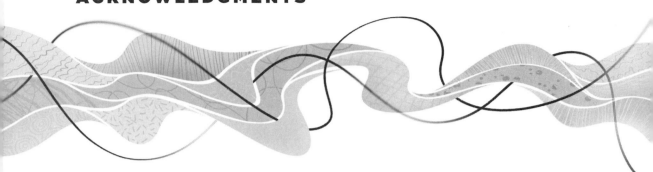

While I wish to acknowledge the recommendations of all those who reviewed the manuscript, I must express particular gratitude to Ron Ballentine, Carol Ann Tomlinson, and Rick Wormeli for their suggestions.

I continue to draw wisdom and understanding from the work of Tom Guskey, Ken O'Connor, Jay McTighe, Douglas Reeves, Rick Stiggins, Grant Wiggins, and Dylan Wiliam. Thank you!

This is my first publication with Solution Tree, and I would like to thank Jeff Jones, Robb Clouse, Stubby McLean, and everyone at this excellent organization for their encouragement and responsiveness.

My access to wonderful schools and stimulating classrooms during this project was made possible through the support of the following leaders and administrators: Jennifer Adams, Lisa Coffey, Heather Gataveckas, Mary Inkster, Steven Massey, Stuart Miller, Jackie Newton, John Stieva, Sandra Sine-Szirtes, and Donna Taylor.

I would be remiss not to acknowledge the exemplary work of the many fine teachers who have contributed, either directly or through example, to this resource. These include Shawn Godin and his mathematics colleagues, Kristin Riddell, Julia Bilenkis, Mary Saunders, Heather Kirk, Adam Lecuyer, C. J. Farmer, Chris Kesner, Sherry Lee, Rosemary Dawson, Karen Ault, Rose Mac-Culloch, Michelle McCutcheon, Kathryn Patterson, Jennifer Brown, Cheryl Clarke, Jodi Cross, Howard Harper, Sheena McGuigan, Nathan Thompson, Andrew Bigham, Ron Marsh, Kate St. Onge, Jennifer Westlake, Rick Olma, Josee Duckett, Cynthia Rhodes-Foley, Lili Stewart, Carolyn Williamson, Holly Miskelly, Michelle Chomniak, Kate Sienna, Claudette Oegema, and Brendan Harman. These remarkable educators work tirelessly to ensure that all children and adolescents in their charge are successful.

And finally, to my partner, Nanci Wakeman, who has read, suggested, questioned, and edited my fuzzy thinking at each stage of the writing process, thank you.

Solution Tree Press would like to thank the following reviewers:

Ron Ballentine
Coordinator, Environmental
    Education, Science, and Technology
Halton District School Board
Burlington, Ontario

Denise Bowling
Assistant Superintendent,
    Instructional Services
Chapel Hill-Carrboro City Schools
Chapel Hill, North Carolina

Susan Brookhart
Author and Consultant
Helena, Montana

Jaime Crowley
Assistant Principal
Mount Hope High School
Bristol, Rhode Island

Glenn Gouthro
Alberta Initiative for School
    Improvement Coordinator
Buffalo Trail Public Schools
Wainwright, Alberta

Tom Hierck
Assistant Superintendent
School District No. 46 (Sunshine
    Coast)
Gibsons, British Columbia

Michelle McCutcheon
Science Teacher
Iroquois Ridge Secondary School
Oakville, Ontario

Sara McGinnis
Curriculum Director
Sheridan County School District #1
Ranchester, Wyoming

Ken O'Connor
Author and Consultant
Scarborough, Ontario

Chris Peek
World History Teacher
Bellaire High School
Bellaire, Texas

Ellen Phillips
Seventh-Grade Social Studies and
    English Teacher
Madeline Symonds Middle School
Hammonds Plains, Nova Scotia

Carol Ann Tomlinson
Professor, Educational Leadership,
    Foundations, and Policy
University of Virginia
Charlottesville, Virginia

Rick Wormeli
Author and Consultant
Herndon, Virginia

Visit **go.solution-tree.com/instruction** to download
reproducibles and other materials associated with this text.

TABLE OF CONTENTS

ABOUT THE AUTHOR

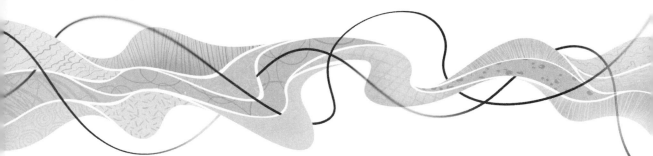

Damian Cooper is an independent consultant who specializes in helping educators in schools and school districts throughout the world improve their instructional and assessment skills. In his varied career, Damian has been a secondary English, special education, and drama teacher; a department head; a librarian; a school consultant; and a curriculum developer. For more than twenty years, he has specialized in student assessment. Damian served as assessment consultant to the School Division of Nelson Education, where he worked on the development of assessment principles and strategies for a wide variety of K–12 resources. He was also coordinator of assessment and evaluation for the Halton District School Board in Burlington, Ontario.

Damian is the author of *Talk About Assessment: Strategies and Tools to Improve Learning* and *Talk About Assessment: High School Strategies and Tools.*

Visit www.damiancooperassessment.com to learn more about Damian's work. To book Damian for professional development, contact pd@solution-tree .com.

FOREWORD

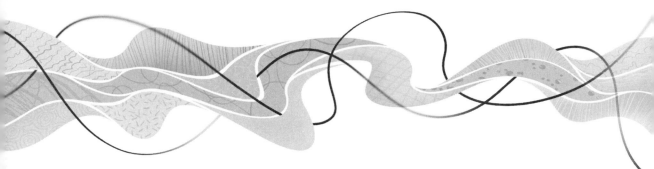

By Michael Fullan

Damian Cooper is a teacher's teacher. He covers every possibility when it comes to differentiated instruction. When you put together the big instructional ideas of the day—differentiation, diverse learners, excellence, equality, assessment, instruction, fairness, and more—you could end up with a lot of clutter. Not Cooper. *Redefining Fair* is at once clear, comprehensive, practical, and action packed. Reading this single book and applying its ideas will make you a better teacher and a better leader of teachers. The book is that good.

Cooper has five imperatives that he carefully honors throughout: curriculum must be meaningful, instruction must be responsive, assessment must be informative, grading must blend consistency and professional judgment, and communication must be truthful and transparent. He proceeds in chapter after chapter to render these concepts crystal clear in terms of their essential qualities and practical uses.

Redefining Fair anticipates and answers every question that any teacher might have about putting differentiation into action: Why is differentiation essential? How do curriculum and assessment connect in a mixed-ability classroom? How do you assess diverse, mixed-ability learners? What is the most effective way to link assessment to instruction in order to get best results? And the big one—what is the best way to handle grading and reporting to students and parents so that grading is seen as both fair and motivating for further learning? With the demand for personalization growing with fierce insistence—partly because too many learners are disengaged, and partly because international assessments have increased the need for more effective teaching (the recent PISA results in the U.S. were called a "Sputnik moment")—teachers are badly in need of instructional ideas that are clear, comprehensive, and effective in engaging the vast majority of diverse students.

Redefining Fair is a treasure trove of great ideas, but it is also focused and coherent. It goes to the heart of teaching in today's classroom. All educators will find this book a spur for immediate action.

This is a book that will keep on giving the more you use it.

Michael Fullan is professor emeritus at the Ontario Institute for Studies in Education of the University of Toronto.

INTRODUCTION

Why This Book Now?

Most teachers I work with now acknowledge the need to differentiate instruction and scaffold assessments to suit the differing strengths and needs of students, but in only a small number of the classes I visit do teachers say that they feel competent or confident in undertaking this work.

In schools, at conferences, and in workshops, teachers constantly tell me that they need help managing the wide range of students they have in their classes. And while the challenges of instruction and assessment are significant, grading and reporting achievement in the mixed-ability classroom often confound even the most experienced professionals. Here are some of the most common questions and concerns voiced when I ask teachers what major challenges they face in assessment and grading:

- How do I differentiate my program for struggling learners when they are all expected to know the same material?

- How should I modify my rubrics for my struggling learners?

- How do I manage my high school classes if I have students moving at different speeds? I have so much to cover.

- I can't insist on all of my students mastering essential learning. At the end of a unit, don't we have to move on?

- How can my report card grades be fair and accurate when I have such a wide range of students in my class?

- How is it fair to those students who are successful the first time if others get to do assignments and tests over again?

- If students know they can do rewrites on major assignments, why should they try the first time?

- If students get to redo tests, won't I have to have lots of tests for every unit?

These are all important, challenging questions. Some involve curriculum, some focus on instruction, some address assessment, and some concern grading. We will explore answers to each of these concerns in the pages of this resource.

Because teaching is such demanding work, requiring the constant integration of wide-ranging knowledge and diverse skills, it frequently overwhelms us. Speaking metaphorically, there are so many individual "trees" demanding our attention—new curriculum to study, lessons to prepare, resources to examine, new skills to learn, school events to organize, teams to coach, and most importantly, individual student needs to meet—that we often lose sight of the "forest"—our overall mission: to teach and assess in ways that maximize learning for *all* students.

The Five Imperatives

Here are five imperatives that should guide our work with respect to curriculum, instruction, assessment, grading, and reporting in the mixed-ability class:

1. Curriculum must be meaningful, coherent, and relevant.

2. Instruction must be responsive to students' needs.

3. Assessment must be informative.

4. Grading must blend consistency with professional judgment.

5. Communication about learning must be truthful and transparent.

The purpose of these imperatives is to present, in as few words as possible, the most important principles for teachers to remember as they undertake the major functions of their role. Each imperative must be unpacked to discover what it looks like in terms of practice. And this "unpacking" comprises the content of this book. For now, let's remove just the first layer of packing material.

1. **Curriculum must be meaningful, coherent, and relevant.**
   What should students be learning in school? This is such a basic question, yet such a difficult one to answer in today's information-saturated world. Given the rate at which knowledge is increasing, educators are wrestling with the question, "What *content* is essential for students to know and understand?" Meanwhile, curriculum

developers are increasingly focusing on broad generic *skills* as the foundation for 21st century learning. As always, the answer to such questions lies not at either extreme of the continuum, but in a balance. And this balance can be achieved only through ongoing dialogue among educators applying the criteria of meaningfulness, coherence, and relevance to inform their decisions.

2. **Instruction must be responsive to students' needs**. Teaching is a craft. Effective teaching is hard work because it demands constant monitoring and adjustment to optimize learning. The teacher's job is *not* to cover the curriculum, regardless of student learning. Rather, it is to understand deeply the intent of the curriculum, and then to use instruction flexibly and adaptively to engage students in ways that maximize learning for all.

3. **Assessment must be informative**. Assessment serves different purposes at different times. One of these purposes—determining what and how well students have learned at the end of an instructional period—receives the most attention but is least important in terms of improving student learning. The first purpose, preassessment, is the starting point for differentiation. Information gleaned from pre-assessment informs teachers and students about areas of strength and areas of need. But the most effective type of assessment is formative—that is, assessment whose purpose is to improve learning. It could be argued that such assessment is indistinguishable from instruction.

4. **Grading must blend consistency with professional judgment**. Grading occurs during brief "time-outs" from teaching and learning. Grading is an accounting process used to summarize large amounts of information about learning into a crude kind of shorthand to let students and their parents know where students stand, relative to known standards. Grading doesn't improve learning—it simply summarizes it. That said, teachers must employ clear, fair, and consistent ways to summarize assessment data and information into grades. But they must also look at each student individually and, when necessary, exercise professional judgment to ensure that report card grades represent the trend in growth, progress, or achievement over time. (I define professional judgment as "decisions made by educators, in light of experience, and with reference to shared public standards and established policies and guidelines.") In short, grades should never come as a surprise

to anyone—neither to the teacher who determines them nor to the students and parents who receive them.

5. **Communication about learning must be truthful and transparent.** Communication about student learning must involve much more than grades. As stated earlier, grades are a form of shorthand. Effective communication with students and their parents involves both formal and informal elements: report cards and parent interviews are formal, whereas telephone, email, and face-to-face conversations, as well as anecdotal notes and commentaries, are informal. All of these communications must be characterized by truthfulness and transparency. These conditions necessitate the separation of information about progress and achievement of knowledge and skills from information about behaviors and attitudes, the use of clearly stated performance standards to describe how learning is measured, and a commitment by teachers to communicate frequently and honestly about every student's learning.

These five imperatives provide the foundation for this resource. In some cases, an imperative applies explicitly to the content of a given chapter. At other times, the imperative is implicit in the messages of the chapter.

Chapter 1 establishes the context for differentiation as a necessary response to the changing demography of schools, to our deepening understanding of how students learn, and to the changing demands of society and the world at large.

Perhaps the greatest obstacles to differentiation of instruction and assessment are outdated beliefs about fairness. As long as fairness is equated with sameness, teachers, students, and parents will perceive variations in teaching and assessment as being unfair. Chapter 2 explores this prevalent and harmful myth and suggests ways to deal with resistance.

As policymakers debate the relative importance of subject content and 21st century skills, teachers continue to struggle with curriculum overload. Chapter 3 examines this issue and suggests that relevance, manageability, and backward design are essential attributes of curriculum planning.

The starting point for differentiated instruction (DI) is a comprehensive process for determining students' needs, interests, and learning preferences. Chapter 4 provides suggestions for how to do this efficiently and effectively.

Effective approaches to differentiation thrive in schools where educators believe in the capacity of all students to be successful and where expectations of excellence underlie the work of both students and teachers. Chapter 5 examines ways to create a culture of excellence in your classroom.

Beginning with a review of norm-, criterion-, and self-referenced assessment, as well as a discussion of growth, progress, and achievement, chapter 6 explains the critical distinction between assessment designed to improve learning (assessment *for* learning) and assessment designed to measure learning (assessment *of* learning) (Stiggins, Arter, Chappuis, & Chappuis, 2004).

Chapter 7 focuses on effective instructional practices. Strategies for empowering students as learning resources to themselves and their peers are presented, as well as recommendations for grouping students, differentiating lessons, and scaffolding learning.

Differentiated assessment requires that teachers understand how to offer students different ways to demonstrate their learning, while maintaining the integrity of the learning targets to be assessed. In chapter 8, we consider how to design assessments that are flexible and responsive to students' strengths, needs, and learning preferences, yet provide evidence of essential learning.

Chapter 9 explores how we should grade learning in the mixed-ability class. While differentiated approaches to instruction and assessment are essential in meeting the needs of all students, the grades used to summarize learning for students and parents must be clear and must be used consistently. That said, teachers must be cognizant of the need for professional judgment when using summary grades to describe achievement or progress.

Few report cards succeed in their intended purpose: to communicate an accurate, succinct, and easily understood summary of learning to students and parents. Chapter 10 examines the different types of information that a report card should communicate and includes recommendations for how reporting may be improved.

The appendix contains reproducible pages that may also be found online. Visit **go.solution-tree.com/instruction** to download these resources.

CHAPTER 1

Why Is Differentiation Essential Today?

The mission of education has changed. Educators and policymakers the world over are coming to understand that everyone benefits when increasing numbers of students graduate from school with the knowledge, skills, and understanding necessary to make meaningful contributions to society. Schools can no longer afford to focus primarily on sifting and sorting students into high, average, and low achievers. Instead, schools must serve to increase the knowledge and skills of *all* children and adolescents.

If the new mission of schools is proficiency for all students, then differentiation is not merely desirable, it is imperative. Most approaches to differentiated instruction identify three broad reasons for adapting teaching to meet the differing needs of students: interest, learning profile, and readiness. These are summarized in the "teacher talk" of figure 1.1 (page 8).

Unfortunately, in many schools that I visit, adapting teaching to students' interests and learning preferences dominates how teachers differentiate instruction. It is extremely rare for me to see teachers collecting and analyzing data about students' strengths and needs with respect to learning and then tailoring instruction strategically on the basis of these data. A far more common practice is requiring students to complete batteries of interest surveys and learning preference questionnaires at the beginning of the school year and then categorizing and labeling students as V/K (visual/kinesthetic), L/M (logical/mathematical), and so on. For the remainder of the year, students find themselves grouped according to their learning preferences and offered choices of learning and assessment tasks based on their interests. Not surprisingly, they tend to pick tasks and topics they like and think will be easy! This is *not* effective differentiated instruction.

Area of Variation	Teacher Talk That Responds to the Variation
Interest	• What are some things that you hope we do during this unit? • On yesterday's exit card, several of you asked how this technique helps architects save time and effort. • For those of you who are interested in finding out more about the fourth state of matter, . . . • I put some magazines on the topic in the resource center. • Some of you raise horses and are wondering how the life cycle of a horse compares to the life cycle of humans. • I want you to research the Spanish-speaking country that you would most like to visit someday. Later, we'll share what we learned in mixed-interest groups. • Darius is planning to show his understanding of balance of powers in the United States by sharing information about the government in his homeland. • Amanda, I've found someone at the local university who is willing to have you work with him in his lab.
Learning Profile	• To write your newsletter, you will need someone who is a good artist, someone who is a good writer, someone who is a good researcher, and someone who is a good organizer. • It doesn't matter to me how you show me that you know the parts of a plant and how they work together to keep the plant healthy. You could tell me, show me, draw a diagram, or write about it. • As long as you choose wisely, you may choose where and with whom to sit. • There are study carrels in the back if you need a quiet space to work. • As long as you do not distract others, you may bring a drink or a snack to eat during class. • To get started with today's work on alliteration in poetry, you may choose to listen to poems that use alliteration, read poems that use alliteration, or write a poem using alliteration. • You may present your final product in front of the class or to me via video or in person by appointment. • Let's think, pair, and then share. • Last week, we broke into teams to see which team knew the most math facts. Today, I want you to work by yourself to improve your score or your time. • You will each take on a different role to debate the effect of current immigration policy.

Figure 1.1: Three variables on which to base differentiation decisions.

Readiness	• Those of you who indicated a need for help in coming up with a topic for your short story, please meet over here, and I will help you brainstorm ideas.
	• If you rated yourself a novice in writing lab reports, start with this assignment. If you rated yourself an apprentice, try this other assignment.
	• If you feel that you have already mastered the material in this chapter, please see me to discuss an alternative project.
	• Please visit those stations that will help you the most as you review for the test.
	• If you have trouble reading and following a map, you will find some bookmarked websites that will help you improve your skills.
	• If you feel that the work I am asking you to do is too hard or too easy, please write me a note.
	• There are vocabulary sheets available for those of you who need them.
	• I have put some sample projects in the back of the room so you can see how other students have approached this assignment in the past.
	• As you think about your independent research topic, browse this journal for some ideas that scientists in the field are currently tackling.
	• I have provided resources that are at varied levels of reading. Please use the techniques we have discussed to help you choose appropriately.

Source: Tools for High-Quality Differentiated Instruction: An ASCD Action Tool *(p. 9), by Cindy A. Strickland, Alexandria, VA: ASCD. © 2007 by ASCD. Reprinted with permission. Learn more about ASCD at www.ascd.org.*

Effective approaches to differentiated instruction require students to work within their zone of proximal development, the zone that challenges without frustrating them, such that their learning is maximized (Vygotsky, 1978). This requires that teachers gather rich preassessment data about students' readiness prior to instruction—data about their prior knowledge and skill levels—and use these data to select entry points for instruction, develop mini lessons for students with similar needs, and adjust instruction on the fly to optimize learning. This aspect of differentiation is by far the most difficult to implement, but I would argue that it is the most important and effective in terms of improving learning.

Taking students' interests and learning profiles into account is an important element of effective instruction, but unless teachers accept that adjusting instruction on the basis of students' strengths and needs is their primary responsibility, no amount of differentiation according to interests and learning profiles will result in increased learning.

The differentiation model is powerful (fig. 1.2) because it places the teacher's response to learners' needs as the starting point for all subsequent decisions. This model also sends an essential message to teachers by placing readiness *before* interests and learning profile.

Teacher Readiness to Implement Differentiated Instruction

Teachers' readiness to implement flexible approaches to curriculum, instruction, and assessment depends on their current skill levels as well as their attitudes toward differentiation. Figure 1.3 (page 12) offers an implementation profile in the form of a continuum that is useful in assisting teachers and administrators in determining readiness with respect to current knowledge and skills. The differentiated instruction continuum may be found online at **go.solution-tree .com/instruction** and in reproducible form in the appendix (page 161).

A continuum is a powerful learning tool because it is descriptive, not evaluative. It enables the learner—in this case, the teacher—to identify current skill levels and to set personal goals for improvement.

However, determining teachers' *attitudinal* readiness to differentiate instruction is more difficult and sensitive. To assist in this area, I go back to the wisdom of David Hunt, a professor from whom I had the privilege of learning while completing a master's degree in education. Dave required all of us to "begin with ourselves" (Hunt, 1987). He asked each of us to identify our personal metaphor of teaching. He then had us explore all new learning we acquired and every decision we made as teachers through this lens. Applying Dave's approach to the essential elements of our craft, we might ask certain kinds of questions. For example, with respect to:

- Curriculum, am I merely the conduit, or am I an architect?
- Instruction, am I the controller or the facilitator of learning?
- Assessment, am I a coach or an accountant?
- Grading, am I a calculator or a professional adjudicator?

By discovering our own metaphor for teaching and then applying it to each of these elements, we can discover a great deal about our readiness to differentiate programs to optimize learning for all students.

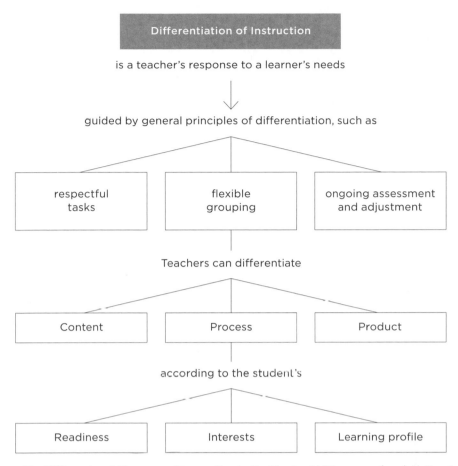

Source: The Differentiated Classroom: Responding to the Needs of All Learners *(p. 15), by Carol Ann Tomlinson, Alexandria, VA: ASCD. © 1999 by ASCD. Reprinted with permission. Learn more about ASCD at www.ascd.org.*

Figure 1.2: Concept map for differentiating instruction.

Three Case Studies

The case studies beginning on page 13, drawn from my own experience as a consultant, highlight distinctly different needs for differentiating programs. The first focuses on an instructional problem, the second on an assessment challenge, and the third on a grading and reporting issue.

PRE-IMPLEMENTATION Developing Instructional Routines and Skills	IMPLEMENTATION Expanding Instructional Routines and Skills	BUILDING CAPACITY Developing the Routines, Habits, and Skills for Differentiated Instruction	SUSTAINING CAPACITY Sustaining a Differentiated Instruction Culture in the Classroom
Modeling to Learners	Shared Practice With Learners	Guided Practice With Learners	Independent Practice With Learners
I design instruction, assessment, evaluation, and the learning environment for the class as a whole based on curriculum expectations and my own strengths and preferences.	I design instruction, assessment, evaluation, and the learning environment based on curriculum expectations and a general sense of the learning needs of the class.	I design instruction, assessment, evaluation, and the learning environment based on curriculum expectations and a general sense of the learning needs of the class. I try to design a variety of options for my students.	I design instruction, assessment, evaluation, and the learning environment based on curriculum expectations and on the specific learning needs of the students in the class. I try to ensure that the learning experiences I provide are a "good fit" for each of my students.
I model while students observe and try to understand.	I work together with students. I model and help students complete the activities.	Students complete the activities while I help them.	Students work independently by adapting my model while I observe.
All students learn and demonstrate their learning in the same way all or most of the time.	Students experience, over time, a variety of ways to learn and/or ways to demonstrate their learning.	Students have a choice of ways to learn and/or ways to demonstrate their learning on an ongoing basis.	Students are routinely provided with, or choose when appropriate, ways to learn and/or ways to demonstrate their learning that are designed for their particular learning needs.
Examples:	**Examples:**	**Examples:**	**Examples:**
Anticipation guide, exit card, graphic organizers, supplementary materials	Activities for all that address different learning styles or intelligences on different days, multiple entry points for all Over time, varied supplementary materials	Differentiation structures that offer choice: centers, Choice Boards, RAFT* assignments Choice of supplementary materials	Differentiation structures such as RAFT* and tiered assignments Provision of, or as appropriate, student choice of supplementary materials based on their needs
Same for all students		**Different options for different students**	
LITTLE DIFFERENTIATION		**MUCH DIFFERENTIATION**	

*RAFT = role, audience, format, topic

© *Queen's Printer for Ontario, 2007. Reproduced with permission.*

Figure 1.3: A differentiated instruction continuum.

Senior History

I was observing a senior grade history class in which the teacher was very proud of her use of differentiated instruction. She had a set of brightly colored index cards that summarized each student's learning modality and preference. During the class, she utilized a number of grouping strategies: students worked at times in home groups and at other times in expert groups, with the latter based on their learning preferences. The climate in the room would best be described as chatty and kinesthetic! Since students spent almost the entire lesson in groups, the teacher felt that she was able to chat with me. However, I quickly discovered that while there were plenty of trappings of DI in place, the learning was superficial at best. The jigsaw (Kagan, 1994) structure was largely ineffective. While in their expert groups, all students read and discussed their assigned text, but once they regrouped in their home groups, it was clear that the other group members had not read anything beyond their own expert group assignment. Consequently, despite the teacher's expectation that there would be sharing and insightful questioning in the home groups, students did not have the necessary background knowledge to be able to do so.

This points to the danger of a superficial understanding of differentiation. Because differentiation requires significant planning and organization before class, teachers often fall into the trap of "too much process, too little learning." Simply assigning students to various groups based on their interests and learning preferences does *not* ensure learning. In fact, such approaches may result in *less* learning than traditional, teacher-centered approaches. In this classroom, whole-class instruction aimed at teaching students strategies for reading and responding to historical texts should have occurred prior to the jigsaw lesson. Furthermore, all students needed to have read all of the texts to ensure that the discussion back in their home groups was productive. And finally, the teacher needed to constantly move from group to group, monitoring and intervening as necessary, to ensure that each group was functioning effectively.

Grade 5 Science

Helen was introducing a project for the following week designed to engage students in independent research about illnesses and diseases affecting human beings.

She spent the greater part of thirty minutes reading and explaining the five-page project outline. Occasionally, she paused and asked, "Are there any questions?" A small number of students asked a few questions. Sitting at the back of the room, I observed as increasing numbers of students became distracted and increasingly disengaged. With just minutes remaining before the lunch recess, Helen issued a few final instructions and then dismissed the class.

We had agreed to chat over lunch. I began by asking, "How did you think that lesson went?"

"I'm ready to quit, Damian," she replied.

"And why is that?"

"Probably two-thirds of my students either won't be able to do a good job on this project or else won't be bothered to. And it's always like this! I'm so frustrated."

I said, "It seems to me that there are three groups in that class. One group that doesn't need a five-page task to get them going—just a clear purpose for the project, an assessment rubric, and a few suggestions, and they'll be off and running. By the way, were the students who asked you questions when you paused in your explanation these self-starters?"

"Yes," Helen replied. "How did you know?"

"I see it all the time." I said. "The students with the questions are usually those who already know what they want to do and how they're going to do it. They're just seeking affirmation. Now, you seem to have another group who could manage if the task were shortened and simplified somewhat. And they'd probably benefit from working in pairs to support each other's learning, especially as they get started. And then there's a group who won't know how to get started, or who will choose not to start, without significant support from you."

"How do you know my class so well? You were in there for only half an hour, and I spent most of that time talking!"

"I'm simply describing most classes I find myself in these days."

"So what do I do?" Helen asked.

"Be proactive. Begin with a common plan for the whole class. This means common, broad learning targets—enduring understandings and essential skills, in the language of Grant Wiggins and Jay McTighe [1998]. And when it comes to assessing the learning, begin with a common design for the task and a common set of assessment criteria. Then, as part of your planning, adapt and modify the task for the different groups of students in your class."

"What does that look like?"

"The self-starters need minimal direction and lots of freedom to explore their own ideas, but within the parameters of the task as you've designed it. The minimal-support group may need the task to be scaffolded. For example, you could reduce the number of resources they are to use and provide an outline of how to conduct their own research, and as I suggested before, you could assign students working partners based on your knowledge of their strengths and needs."

"What about the weakest group?"

"They need to begin by working directly under your supervision. You'll need to scaffold the task still further for them and do plenty of review of the foundational knowledge and skills required by this project. What I'm talking about is a blueprint for assessment task design that begins with an overall common design for the task but also includes accommodations, modifications, and scaffolding that will enable the various groups in your class to be successful."

"But isn't this just ability grouping, which I thought we aren't supposed to do?"

"Good question. The problem with ability grouping was that students tended to become stuck in the group they were assigned to. The result, as you know, were the 'eagles,' 'sparrows,' and 'crows' that served only to consign large numbers of students to a school career of drill-and-kill drudgery. With effective differentiation, the composition of the groups I've described will change constantly. In the differentiated classroom, your goal is to have all students produce excellent work that reflects mastery of essential learning and to have them do so independently. But to get all students to this point, you will need to employ the kinds of strategies we've been discussing."

Helen left our lunchtime chat feeling encouraged and positive about her class. And I wasn't afraid that she might quit!

This case study reflects a problem that I encounter almost daily in elementary, middle, and high schools: students are clustered in a classroom that is identified as one grade level (in this case, grade 5). Our standards-based models of curriculum and grading emphasize that all students enrolled in this class are expected to master a prescribed set of skills and understand a set of concepts by the end of the year. In other words, learning has been defined in terms of seat time, rather than demonstrated understanding and proficiency, with little consideration given to the range of students in the class.

Helen had been constrained by the "learning-as-a-function-of-seat-time" model, which she had interpreted to mean one size must fit all. She also felt constrained by all the curriculum outcomes that she had to cover, and the thought of differentiating her approach for groups within the class invoked panic and desperation. She needed a process and format to help her design assessment tasks for her mixed-ability class.

Grade 10 Mathematics

The high school mathematics department heads in a large Canadian school district had become increasingly dissatisfied with student results in their schools. These were their major concerns:

- Unacceptably high, as well as highly variable, failure rates on end-of-semester examinations—for example, a 50 percent failure rate on the January examination and a 5 percent failure rate in June. The exams were similar and created by the same people, the only difference being the way they were graded.

- Numbers of students receiving passing grades at the end of a course, despite having shown little or no understanding of some of the key concepts or little or no evidence of some of the essential skills in a given course.

In the province of Ontario, all assessment must occur with reference to a four-level performance standard. However, report card grades must be expressed as percentages, and 50 percent is the pass/fail threshold. The Ministry of Education provides teachers with the scale shown in figure 1.4 to align the four levels of performance with percentage grade ranges.

Because it did not appear that the Ministry of Education was about to raise the 50 percent cut point for pass/fail, these educators set themselves the following challenge: how can we assure students and parents that a final grade of 50 percent in a mathematics course means that the student has demonstrated minimal mastery of all of the essential learning in that course? Their initial thinking (this is a work in progress) was as follows:

> To get a credit in grade 10 academic (college level) mathematics, *all* of the overall expectations (learning outcomes or standards) must be demonstrated to a minimum of Level 1. This work is an attempt

Percentage Mark	Achievement of the Provincial Curriculum Expectations
80-100	The student has demonstrated the required knowledge and skills with a high degree of effectiveness. Achievement surpasses the provincial standard. (Level 4)
70-79	The student has demonstrated the required knowledge and skills with considerable effectiveness. Achievement meets the provincial standard. (Level 3)
60-69	The student has demonstrated the required knowledge and skills with some effectiveness. Achievement approaches the provincial standard. (Level 2)
50-59	The student has demonstrated the required knowledge and skills with limited effectiveness. Achievement falls much below the provincial standard. (Level 1)
Below 50	The student has not demonstrated the required knowledge and skills. Extensive remediation is required.
I	Insufficient evidence to assign a percentage mark (for grade 9 and 10 courses only)
W	The student has withdrawn from this course.
ESL/ELD—Achievement is based on expectations modified from the curriculum for the course to support English-language learning needs.	
IEP—Individual Education Plan **French**—The student receives instruction in French for the course.	
SHSM—Specialist High Skills Major (for grade 11 and 12 courses only) **Course Median**—The median is the percentage mark at which 50 percent of the students have a higher percentage mark and 50 percent of the students have a lower percentage mark.	

© *Queen's Printer for Ontario, 2010. Reproduced with permission.*

Figure 1.4. Aligning four levels of performance with percentage grades.

to articulate the bottom-line for each overall expectation: what is the least students can show us and still get credit? We hope this will seed a discussion, rather than being the final word!!

One of the criticisms of the new model for evaluation in math is that students will get a credit when they shouldn't. The articulation below should give us confidence that the students have achieved some level of understanding in *all* topics in the course— as compared to the past, where students could earn a grade 10 academic credit with virtually no understanding of quadratics, for example, because they could earn enough marks in trigonometry or analytic geometry to earn a grade of 50 percent.

As in the past, there will still be students who earn credit but are apparently not ready for grade 11 academic level math. Again, we must emphasize that while they have the right to take any course for which they have a prerequisite—and in some cases even when they don't—students should not consider themselves ready for the next course at the same level unless they have achieved Level 3 or 4 in the prerequisite course.

Here are some of the ways that final grades may be determined.

- Use multiple and varied opportunities for students to demonstrate the threshold requirement for each overall expectation to earn the credit. A final grade of 45 percent in a course would indicate that only one of the overall expectations is absent and that the credit could be recovered by addressing that expectation. A final grade of less than 45 percent would indicate more comprehensive gaps.

- Use multiple and varied opportunities to assign a level of achievement for each cluster of overall expectations in a strand. (Assign the most recent or consistent level.) Use the lowest of the levels achieved for each of the strands as a starting point, and then modify upward (within that level or the next at the low end) by looking at the other strands.

- Exams and other summative assessments should be viewed as final opportunities to demonstrate and confirm the levels of achievement by students throughout the course.

- A Level 3 rating requires that students demonstrate all of the overall expectations to a considerable degree.

- A Level 4 rating requires attaining a minimum of Level 4 in all strands, as well as consistent and thorough demonstration of the overall expectations. (S. Godin, personal communication, February 18, 2010)

I applaud the work of these mathematics educators as they struggle to address the pervasive problem of students' and parents' believing that a grade of 50 percent is good enough. Their work is one of the best examples I have seen of aligning percentage grades with clearly understood public statements of proficiency—meaningful grades. All students and all parents deserve grades that accurately and truthfully summarize what students have learned, and by implication, what they have not learned.

This case study identifies a common district-level problem: large numbers of students are poorly served and often failed by a curriculum that was designed by academic experts for only a portion of the population—university-bound students. This example also highlights the limitations of a points-based, percentage-grade system when applied to a standards-based curriculum purportedly designed to ensure that students acquire essential skills and understanding. Such an unhappy marriage of two conflicting paradigms—one designed to sift and sort students into high, average, and low achievers, and the other to certify the proficiency of all—inevitably leads to a situation in which some students who may have learned a great deal still "fail" the course, while others "pass," despite the fact that there are huge gaps in their learning!

In subsequent chapters we examine the kinds of challenges reflected in these three case studies.

Conclusion

Differentiation, or *responsive teaching* (Tomlinson & McTighe, 2006)—a term I use increasingly instead of differentiation, as many teachers react negatively to what they regard as the latest panacea—is a response by the educational community to 21st century demands that *all* learners leave school equipped with the knowledge and skills they will need to function in an ever-changing global community. While many teachers have not been trained specifically in differentiation methods, all educators have a professional responsibility to develop the knowledge and skills necessary to meet the needs of diverse learners.

Differentiated instruction is much more complex than simply offering students choices with respect to how they will learn and how they will demonstrate their learning. While determining students' interests and learning preferences is necessary to optimize learning, the most important, albeit most challenging, task facing the teacher in the mixed-ability class involves determining students' current knowledge and skill levels and adjusting instruction accordingly. Teachers' success in undertaking this task depends on their own current skill levels, as well as their willingness to be flexible in terms of differentiating both instruction and assessment.

CHAPTER 2

What Does "Fair" Mean in the Mixed-Ability Class?

"Is it fair to students who are successful the first time if others get to do assignments and tests over again?" "If students know they can do rewrites on major assignments, why would they try the first time, knowing they can just do it again?" "If students get to redo tests, won't I have to create lots of tests for every unit?"

Heard these questions before? I hear them constantly! Clearly, we must re-examine our notions of fairness, given that despite an ever-widening range of prior learning in today's classrooms, teachers are expected to ensure that all students acquire essential learning.

Debunking the Bell Curve

I draw on my love of cycling to illustrate for educators, students, and parents what instruction, assessment, and grading must look like to ensure high-quality learning from all students. Traditional models of schooling can be compared to a stage in the Tour de France. Simply put, the Tour de France is a one-size-fits-all model in which riders compete against each other, against the clock, over the exact same distance, taking the exact same route. There is only one place on the podium at the end of each stage. The majority of riders finish in the peloton. They don't reach the podium, but they complete the course, and they all receive the same time for that day's stage. Typically, in each stage of the three-week race, some riders fail to finish in the required time and are out of the race.

Sound familiar? This is analogous to covering the curriculum once, in the same way, for all students, periodically stopping to test what has been learned. Students compete for a fixed and limited number of "A" grades. Only a few make the podium. The majority of students master some of the material covered and receive average grades—the peloton. Some students fail the test, and while they may continue in the course or grade, they fall progressively further behind and eventually find themselves out of the race. The point of this exercise? To sift and sort students into high, average, and low achievers for the purpose of determining placement in one of three program levels, with the ultimate purpose being to determine postsecondary destinations.

In this model, time constraints permit only superficial, one-time coverage of the curriculum. And the teacher is unlikely to provide performance standards for assessment tasks, because to do so would likely result in too many students achieving "A" grades. Similarly, the teacher does not differentiate instruction or assessment based on differing student needs, because, again, to do so, would likely alter the desired normal distribution of grades. But today's information-rich, digital world demands high levels of literacy, numeracy, and problem solving from *all* students.

So what should a 21st century model of instruction, assessment, and grading look like? Instead of the Tour de France, it needs to resemble a guided bicycle tour. On a bicycle tour, the guide has the route for the day's ride and starts out by leading the way. But the riders don't necessarily stay together, so throughout the ride, the guide doubles back to check on all the riders. She ensures that no one is riding alone, that everyone is cycling at his or her own comfort level, and that no one gets lost or overwhelmed by the terrain. When the guide discovers that some riders have dismounted from their bikes and are looking skeptically at a particularly steep hill, she says, "You don't have to climb it. Let me show you an alternate route." Of course, all riders make it to the picturesque country inn by the end of the day, where each celebrates his or her accomplishment over a fine meal! Some have taken a different route; some have taken longer than others to arrive at their destination; but all riders have participated in a ride that is appropriate to their skill and fitness levels.

This is today's differentiated classroom. As educators, we must learn to run our classrooms and schools according to the guided bicycle tour model, rather than the Tour de France model.

The following classroom is an exemplar of the "guided bicycle tour" approach.

Holly's Grade 8 Language Arts

Holly has a class of thirty-one students who demonstrate a wide range of interests, skills, and motivation to learn, but the learning targets for her language arts lesson are the same for all:

- Making Inferences/Interpreting Texts

  1.5 develop and explain interpretations of oral texts using the language of the text and oral and visual cues to support their interpretations. (p. 141)

- Metacognition

  3.1 identify what strategies they found most helpful before, during, and after listening and speaking and what steps they can take to improve their oral communication skills. (p. 140)

  © *Queen's Printer for Ontario, 2006. Reproduced with permission.*

A short play about sibling rivalry called *Sibling Secrets* (Hume & Ledgerwood, 2008) provides the focus for Holly's language arts lesson. At the beginning of the term, she used a variety of diagnostic assessment strategies to determine the skill levels of her students. Because today's task involves reading, she has relied upon data from a developmental reading assessment (DRA) to group students strategically. Her lesson plan follows a simple yet effective format:

1. Activation of prior knowledge—whole class
2. Pre-reading activities to stimulate interest and alert students to text features—whole class
3. Oral reading of text—heterogeneous groups
4. Debriefing of text—whole class
5. Analysis of text and making inferences—homogeneous groups

Each of the heterogeneous groups for task 3 comprises three students of differing reading skill levels. The intent is that the more skilled readers will assist the less skilled as they read the text aloud together. Holly moves from group to group to monitor their reading and to provide assistance as necessary.

The homogeneous groups for task 5 comprise students of approximately the same reading skill levels. Holly provides each group with a differentiated task related to inferencing.

Holly's lesson and assessment rubric may be downloaded at **go.solution -tree.com/instruction** and found in reproducible form in the appendix (pages 162–168).

Much like the bicycle tour guide leader, Holly has a clear sense of the destination of all of her students. Also like the tour guide, she has taken the time to assess their differing levels of skill and experience, and she uses this information to make critical decisions that will ensure that every student is appropriately challenged and, therefore, learning.

Retries: Lowering or Raising Standards?

Rick Wormeli (2006) reminds us that "fair isn't always equal." The greatest obstacles to treating students differently on the basis of differing needs are habit and tradition. In no other professional endeavor involving practitioners and human beings would we condone treating everyone in the same way. Imagine the doctor who prescribed the same medicine to all patients, regardless of their symptoms, or the physiotherapist who utilized the same treatment for every injury! We would consider such practitioners unworthy of the term *professional.* Yet in education, we have come to equate the concept of rigor in teaching with sameness. Hence, we hear comments such as, "It's not fair to those students who are successful the first time if others get to do assignments and tests over again." The problem with this argument is that it is focused on the teacher. Instead, we must hold *students* accountable to rigorous standards. Instead of *allowing* retakes, we must *demand* retakes by students if their first attempt does not meet prescribed performance standards.

This is a radical shift in perspective, in which student, teacher, and parent come to see the insistence on quality work from all as a reflection of *higher,* not lower standards.

Unfortunately, we face a massive public relations challenge to convince parents, postsecondary institutions, and the media that requiring students to improve and resubmit substandard work does *not* equate to "being soft on students" or offering them a "no-consequences education" (Wente, 2009). On the contrary, these practices represent a significant raising of the bar. But most parents, postsecondary institutions, and the media embrace a norm-referenced or "sift and sort" model of assessment and grading. They either are unfamiliar with or do not understand why the 21st century demands criterion-referenced assessment and grading practices—practices that specify what excellence looks like, and why we must settle for nothing less from every student.

How can educators change the perception widely held among parents, the community, and the media that "retakes," "redos," and second and third attempts, far from being easy on students, do, in fact reflect higher standards? Everyone inside and outside the educational community needs to understand that two fundamental changes are occurring:

1. The mission of K–12 schooling has changed from sifting and sorting students into winners and losers to educating *all* students to be highly skilled and knowledgeable with respect to essential learning.

2. This change requires that students' learning be assessed and graded, not by comparison to each other, but against a prescribed set of standards.

When speaking with teachers and parent groups, I use the analogy of driver certification to illustrate these changes. "How many of you passed your in-car driving test the first time?" I ask. As the hands are raised and the laughing begins, I ask, "How many of you yelled 'Not fair!' when your neighbor had to take his or her test three times before passing?" The fact is, no one wants to share the road with that person until he or she passes the test, even if it takes ten tries! This isn't going soft on drivers—this is demanding proficiency.

As an email I received from a consultant in Coquitlam, British Columbia, indicates, demanding proficiency from students is achievable! She wrote:

> Thirty educators have applied to be part of our action research learning teams working in a facilitated model, where they do evidence-based inquiry into the difference that applying your ideas makes to the learning of their students. The short-term outcomes are already amazing. One secondary English department made 75 percent the minimum achievement in all of its classes and is utilizing any number of formative assessment practices to ensure this level of learning occurs. (J. Reid, personal communication, December 8, 2008. Used with permission.)

Countering Resistance in the Classroom

I have seen, both as a teacher and consultant, that when teachers believe that one size does not fit all, and when all of their words and actions model equity of opportunity, students, including those in the senior grades, quickly come on board. The complaint that "it's not fair to those who succeed the first time when others get second and third chances" rarely comes from students. It is an attitude most commonly acquired from teachers. However, when teachers engage their students in conversation about what's fair, and when they use examples and analogies such as the bicycle tour and the driver's test to illustrate common practice outside of school, it *is* possible to create a culture of excellence in the classroom.

The teachers in the three case studies that follow embrace this concept of fairness.

Mike's Mathematics Class

During the last few weeks of the semester, Mike spends a good portion of instructional time reviewing the key learnings from the entire course, in order to set his students up for success on their final examination. Key to this review is having his students develop their own, personalized review guide. Once Mike has led the class in reviewing a particular concept or procedure, he sets students to work at computers to add information about this material to their individual review guides. Some students favor graphic organizers such as mind maps, concept webs, or Venn diagrams; others favor jotting notes. Some record their material in traditional linear style, while others' review guides resemble doodles! Most importantly, however, each student creates a guide that will best serve his or her own learning style and that will prove most helpful, personally, during the exam. (Yes, students take their review guides into the examination room!)

"Surely that is akin to letting them cheat," I hear some teachers say. But Mike has compared results over time, including occasions when he did not permit students to take their review sheets into the examination room and found there to be no significant difference in achievement on the examination. He has also found that, since requiring students to create their own review sheets instead of providing one for them, their understanding of mathematics has increased significantly. In his words, "The learning happens as students are putting their review sheet together."

Mike and his colleagues are committed to teaching and assessing for deep understanding, not simple memorization of mathematical procedures. Hence, in addition to the final examination, they gather evidence of students' mathematical understanding through open-ended performance tasks, math logs, and individual conferences with students. These assessments are designed to assess whether students can select from what they have learned and apply the appropriate concepts and procedures when faced with new problems. These teachers have little need for secure tests that are sealed in envelopes until examination day; such assessments tend to favor those students who are most adept at memorizing endless formulas. Instead, Mike's assessments measure what students can do with what they have learned by focusing on essential skills, including problem solving, critical thinking, and communication.

Michelle M.'s Science Class

Michelle M. teaches two grade 10 science classes: one is a gifted cluster class, and the other comprises a broad range of students. She is committed to differentiation and gathers a wealth of diagnostic information about her students' learning readiness, learning preferences, and interests. On the day I visited her two classes, Michelle was preparing her students for an end-of-unit test on light. The "essential questions" (Wiggins & McTighe, 1998) that both classes had investigated during the unit included:

- What is light?
- How is light reflected and refracted?
- How do reflection and refraction affect us in our daily lives?

Michelle had set up stations throughout her classroom, reflecting a full range of learning styles and multiple intelligences. Here are some examples:

> **Station #2:** Turn on the overhead projector, then view the happy face through the pinhole camera.
>
> 1. What are the characteristics of the image?
> 2. What can you do to make the image larger than the object? Smaller than the object? The same size?

3. Provide your answers to #2 using a mathematical formula.

Station #4: Use the ray box and concave/convex mirrors provided to answer the following:

1. How does light reflect differently off concave and convex mirrors?

2. Draw ray diagrams to illustrate your observations.

3. What kind of mirror would truck drivers want as a rearview mirror to help see vehicles in their blind spot? Explain and use a diagram to support your answer.

As we chatted, Michelle made an interesting observation about the difference between the gifted and the regular class:

> The students in this gifted cluster class tend to choose review tasks that involve reading and writing, and I had to encourage many of them to move to the hands-on stations, whereas most of the students in the regular class head straight for the hands-on stations, and I have to encourage them to complete some of the writing tasks. (M. McCutcheon, personal communication, March 8, 2010)

Michelle's comment points to one of the teacher's primary responsibilities regarding students' learning styles and preferences: encouraging students to move out of their comfort zone in order to broaden their skills and knowledge. However, doing so is not always popular with students. A girl in the gifted cluster class told me that she was often frustrated in Ms. McCutcheon's class:

> I like to just learn from the textbook and then just study for tests. But she makes us do work stations, and she makes us debate different points of view.

My hope is that Michelle and this student will discuss these frustrations and reach an understanding about the benefits of learning in a variety of ways.

Michelle C.'s Mathematics Class

Michelle C. finds that in her mathematics class the interactive whiteboard engages many students who would previously have been reluctant learners. Today's lesson begins with a preassessment to determine her students' current understanding of congruence and similarity as applied to two-dimensional figures. She calls students individually, or in pairs, to come to the board to move a variety of figures into either the "congruent" or "similar" column on the board, relative to a reference figure. During this process, she notes which students are correct and confident in their placement of figures and which are not. On the basis of this data, she convenes a small group to work directly with her, using manipulatives to address their confusion. Meanwhile, other groups continue to work at the interactive whiteboard, categorizing more complex shapes such as pentagons and octagons.

Later in the lesson, Michelle wants to encourage as many students as possible to begin to work independently on problems. At this point, she turns their attention to the Traffic Lights (Black, Harrison, Lee, Marshall, & Wiliam, 2003) poster on the wall (fig. 2.1), a self-assessment tool to help students determine their readiness to work independently. Michelle designs sets of questions or other assessment tasks to suit each of the levels on the poster. Students identifying their level as green will work independently on more challenging tasks or questions, students selecting yellow will undertake moderately challenging work and may seek help from a peer at any time, and students identifying their level as red will continue to work with Michelle in a small group.

Although she occasionally has to intervene when a student makes an inappropriate choice, Michelle finds that, as the year progresses, students become progressively more accurate in determining their level of independence.

Green	Yellow	Red
I feel like this is a walk in the park.	I feel like I know what I'm doing.	I feel like I don't know what to do.
I feel great.	I feel good.	I feel frustrated.
I am very comfortable with this.	I understand, but it would help if I could discuss further if I have problems.	I am confused and need to talk further about this.

Figure 2.1: "Traffic lights" student self-assessment chart.

Traffic lighting is a powerful "assessment *as* learning" strategy (Earle, 2004). Assessment *as* learning engages students in self-assessment to develop their metacognitive skills. By routinely using the traffic-light chart, Michelle is teaching her students to constantly monitor their current levels of skill and understanding, to set new goals that reflect an appropriate challenge, and to constantly adjust what they think and do in order to achieve these goals.

Conclusion

Fairness in today's mixed-ability classroom is not achieved through "one-size-fits-all" approaches. Fairness must be redefined in terms of equity of opportunity. Students are individuals, and excellence in education must be defined in terms of all students realizing their potential—not all students learning the same things, in the same way, in the same amount of time. Some students will require more time than others; some will need more than one attempt to be successful. For these changes to occur across schools, districts, states, and provinces, teachers, students, parents, and society at large must reconceptualize success in terms of *all* students demonstrating proficiency with respect to essential learning.

Educators face a significant challenge in this regard. Current misconceptions among many students, parents, the media—and many teachers—include the belief that retakes of tests and revisions to substandard work represent an erosion of standards. In fact, they represent a raising of standards. The educational community must step up to the plate and change the message. Instead of "second chances" and "opportunities to redo work," we must use phrases such as "I demand high-quality work from all of my students," and "This school insists upon excellence." School culture must change to embrace a commitment to success for all and an acceptance that this goal requires a flexible and responsive approach to instruction and assessment.

CHAPTER 3

How Should Curriculum and Assessment Connect in the Mixed-Ability Class?

Curriculum is the "what" of teaching. The origin of the word is the Latin *currere,* meaning "to run." Hence, the curriculum represents the course we require students to run on their journey to learning. Few would argue that curriculum must be dynamic, as it must be constantly under examination and review to ensure that it reflects an ever-changing world. That said, curriculum should reflect certain fundamental concepts and essential skills that are timeless. Fundamental concepts—what Wiggins and McTighe (1998) call "enduring understandings"—include, for example, the laws of gravity and energy conservation in science and the archetypal narrative patterns and characters in world literature. Essential skills include problem solving in all domains and argumentative discourse in the humanities. These critical learnings will continue to provide the foundation for curriculum in such subject areas.

However, the overarching question challenging curriculum developers in the 21st century is: what should be the balance of knowledge and skills in today's curriculum? The Partnership for 21st Century Skills in the United States proposes a framework (fig. 3.1, page 32) to address this question.

Core Subjects and 21st Century Themes

- English, reading, or language arts
- World languages
- Arts
- Mathematics
- Economics
- Science
- Geography
- History
- Government and civics

21st Century Interdisciplinary Themes

- Global awareness
- Financial, economic, business, and entrepreneurial literacy
- Civic literacy
- Health literacy
- Environmental literacy

Learning and Innovation Skills

- Creativity and innovation
- Critical thinking and problem solving
- Communication and collaboration

Information, Media, and Technology Skills

- Information literacy
- Media literacy
- ICT literacy

Life and Career Skills

- Flexibility and adaptability
- Initiative and self-direction
- Social and cross-cultural skills
- Productivity and accountability
- Leadership and responsibility

Source: Framework for 21st Century Learning, *by the Partnership for 21st Century Skills, 2006. Reprinted with permission.*

Figure 3.1: The framework for learning proposed in the United States.

This model seeks to strike a balance of traditional subject content (English, mathematics, and so on), interdisciplinary content (global awareness and health literacy, for example), and three sets of skills (learning and innovation; information, media, and technology; and life and career).

At the state level, New Jersey's 2009 curriculum framework may be seen as an attempt to integrate the digital and technological demands of the 21st century with traditional content areas:

> New Jersey's 2009 Core Curriculum Content Standards address two critical education priorities. The revised standards align with the knowledge and skills needed by all students for post-secondary opportunities, which may encompass: four-year college, community college, technical training, military service, direct entry into the workplace, and an array of future careers—including some that are just being envisioned and others that are currently unforeseen. In addition, the standards by necessity reflect a framework for teaching and learning that responds to the needs of 21st-century digital learners by incorporating the 'new literacies' required in an innovation economy: the ability to effectively access, evaluate, and synthesize vast amounts of information; to apply knowledge and skills to personal, workplace, and global challenges; to work collaboratively in cross-cultural settings; to solve problems creatively; and to act ethically as citizens of the world community.
>
> These 21st-century student outcomes require a deeper understanding of academic content at much higher levels than ever before. The revised standards facilitate this in-depth learning in all content areas through the systematic and transparent integration of 21st-century knowledge, skills, and themes; global perspectives; cross content connections; and technology. Consequently, successful implementation of the revised standards requires rethinking of traditional curricular and assessment approaches, as well as the creation of 21st-century learning environments in which teachers and students work across and beyond traditional disciplines and boundaries as engaged co-learners, critical and creative thinkers, and problem solvers.
>
> K-12 standards for: Visual and Performing Arts; Comprehensive Health and Physical Education; Science; Social Studies; World Languages; Technology; and 21st-Century Life and Careers, Standards for Mathematics and Language Arts Literacy are part of the Common Core State Standards initiative (www.corestandards.org) coordinated by the Council of Chief State School Officers (CCSSO) and the National Governors Association (NGA) in partnership with other national organizations. New Jersey is one of 50 states to join the state-led Common Core State Standards initiative. (New Jersey Department of Education, 2009)

These two examples of curriculum reform—one at the national level and one at the state level—illustrate the current tension between the demands of our digital, technology-driven world and our historical commitment to traditional subject domains. I would argue that because knowledge is almost universally available to North American and Canadian students via the Internet, a 21st century curriculum should focus more on essential skills than on content knowledge. I would argue, furthermore, that since knowledge is transmitted more easily via information technology than skills, teachers are more critical to the learning and refinement of skills than they are to the acquisition of knowledge.

Robert Sternberg's work echoes this belief, as evidenced by his "Other 3 Rs." After a two-year pilot study funded by the James S. McDonnell Foundation, he and his colleagues suggest the curriculum framework illustrated in figure 3.2.

These three markedly different 21st century curriculum frameworks illustrate the intense debate that is currently underway concerning what students should be learning in school.

Clearly, curriculum documents currently in use across the United States and Canada contain far more content than teachers can ever hope to cover, let alone expect students to learn. To address this problem, the seminal work of Wiggins and McTighe is helping to liberate teachers from the tyranny of curriculum overload. More importantly, their "backward design" (Wiggins & McTighe, 1998) approach is helping students focus their learning efforts on the knowledge and skills that are essential to help them lead fulfilling, responsible, and productive lives.

Planning With the End in Mind

As Tomlinson points out (2001), differentiated instruction does not mean thirty different lesson plans each day for each of the students in your class. The key to planning curriculum and instruction in the mixed-ability class is to identify essential learning for all students. This is why the backward design model is not only a good idea; it is, I suggest, the *only* way teachers today can cope with curriculum overload.

Defining the Other 3 Rs: Reasoning, Resilience, and Responsibility

- Reasoning—thinking that utilizes explicit and/or implicit rules, with this program focusing on effective problem solving, particularly in regard to academic challenges.
    + Rules—"If I am going to think clearly about solving a problem (or reaching a goal) I need clear rules to follow."
- Resilience—competently surmounting challenges, both inside and outside of school.
    + Challenges and difficulties are a normal part of life—"Challenges are normal. We all have them."
    + Persistence/determination—"If at first I don't succeed I will try again." (A cautionary note for this message is that people can take their determination to an extreme and become obsessive about reaching a goal. Encourage students to find a balance.)
    + View obstacles as challenges to be overcome (approach challenges by keeping things in perspective and seeing them as opportunities for learning).
        - "What can I learn from this?"
- Responsibility—being accountable for one's own actions and inactions and the consequences of those actions and inactions.
    + Personal responsibility
        - "It's up to me to create what I want."
        - "It's up to me to make it happen."
        - "How I act matters."
    + Academic responsibility
        - "Good grades result from my efforts."
        - "If I want to learn it is up to me."
        - "If I don't understand, I have to ask."
    + Social responsibility
        - Considering other peoples' points of view—"I care about what you have to say."
        - Concern for the common good—"I care about what is good for all of us, not just for me."
        - Giving help and seeking help—"I will help you." "I need help."

Source: The Other 3 Rs: Reasoning, Resilience, and Responsibility. Copyright © 2004 by the American Psychological Association. Reproduced with permission. No further reproduction or distribution is permitted without written permission from the American Psychological Association.

Figure 3.2: The other 3 Rs: reasoning, resilience, and responsibility.

Let's begin by examining why curriculum coverage by the teacher is not only a misguided approach but also an impossible task. Consider the example of grade 5 social studies standards in figure 3.3.

Students should be able to: Apply concepts and skills learned in previous grades.

HISTORY AND GEOGRAPHY

1. Identify different ways of dating historical narratives (17th century, 1600s, colonial period).

2. Interpret timelines of events studied.

3. Observe and identify details in cartoons, photographs, charts, and graphs relating to historical narrative.

4. Use maps and globes to identify absolute locations (latitude and longitude).

5. Identify the location of the North and South Poles, the equator, the prime meridian, Northern, Southern, Eastern, and Western Hemispheres.

6. Distinguish between political and topographical maps and identify specialized maps that show information such as population, income, or climate change.

7. Compare maps of the modern world with historical maps of the world before the Age of Exploration, and describe the changes in 16th and 17th century maps of the world.

Figure 3.3: Grade 5 concepts and skills.

Although only a partial list, this represents a reasonable set of skills for students in grade 5 to master. Now let's examine what they are actually expected to know (fig. 3.4).

The set of content standards in figures 3.3 and 3.4 represent less than 50 percent of the history and geography content that students in grade 5 in the state of Massachusetts are expected to know, to say nothing of the endless lists of standards in the other subjects! If ever there were a curriculum in need of big ideas and essential skills, this is it! The science example from Florida in figure 3.5 (page 38) is far less daunting.

These broad learning targets include a manageable number of enduring understandings about energy. Because the last four targets include the word *investigate,* they imply that students will also demonstrate skills of scientific inquiry as they come to understand the concepts.

PRE-COLUMBIAN CIVILIZATIONS OF THE NEW WORLD AND EUROPEAN EXPLORATION, COLONIZATION, AND SETTLEMENT TO 1700

Building on knowledge from previous years, students should be able to:

5.1 Describe the earliest explorations of the New World by the Vikings, the period and locations of their explorations, and the evidence for them. (H, G)

5.2 Identify the three major pre-Columbian civilizations that existed in Central and South America (Maya, Aztec, and Inca) and their locations. Describe their political structures, religious practices, and use of slaves. (H, G, E)

5.3 Explain why trade routes to Asia had been closed in the 15th century and trace the voyages of at least four of the explorers listed below. Describe what each explorer sought when he began his journey, what he found, and how his discoveries changed the image of the world, especially the maps used by explorers. (H, G, E)

   A. Vasco Núñez de Balboa   F. Henry Hudson
   B. John and Sebastian Cabot   G. Ferdinand Magellan
   C. Jacques Cartier   H. Juan Ponce de León
   D. Samuel de Champlain   I. Amerigo Vespucci
   E. Christopher Columbus

5.4 Explain why the Aztec and Inca civilizations declined in the 16th century. (H)

   A. The encounters between Cortez and Montezuma
   B. The encounters between Pizarro and the Incas
   C. The goals of the Spanish conquistadors
   D. The effects of European diseases, particularly smallpox, throughout the Western hemisphere

5.5 Describe the goals and extent of the Dutch settlement in New York, the French settlements in Canada, and the Spanish settlements in Florida, the Southwest, and California. (H)

5.6 Explain the early relationship of the English settlers to the indigenous peoples, or Indians, in North America, including the differing views on ownership or use of land and the conflicts between them (e.g., the Pequot and King Philip's Wars in New England). (H, G, E)

5.7 Identify some of the major leaders and groups responsible for the founding of the original colonies in North America. (H, C)

   A. Lord Baltimore in Maryland   D. Roger Williams in Rhode Island
   B. William Penn in Pennsylvania   E. John Winthrop in Massachusetts
   C. John Smith in Virginia

5.8 Identify the links between the political principles and practices developed in ancient Greece and such political institutions and practices as written constitutions and town meetings of the Puritans. (H, C)

5.9 Explain the reasons that the language, political institutions, and political principles of what became the United States of America were largely shaped by English colonists even though other major European nations also explored the New World. (H, C)

   A. The relatively small number of colonists who came from other nations besides England
   B. Long experience with self-government
   C. The high rates of literacy and education among the English colonial leaders
   D. England's strong economic, intellectual, and military position

Source: Massachusetts History and Social Science Curriculum Framework, *by the Massachusetts Department of Education, 2003.*

Figure 3.4: Grade 5 learning standards from Massachusetts.

> **Big Idea 10: Forms of Energy**
>
> A. Energy is involved in all physical processes and is a unifying concept in many areas of science.
>
> B. Energy exists in many forms and has the ability to do work or cause a change.
>
> SC.5.P.10.1: Investigate and describe some basic forms of energy, including light, heat, sound, electrical, chemical, and mechanical.
> Depth of Knowledge: Moderate
>
> SC.5.P.10.2: Investigate and explain that energy has the ability to cause motion or create change.
> Depth of Knowledge: High
>
> SC.5.P.10.3: Investigate and explain that an electrically charged object can attract an uncharged object and can either attract or repel another charged object without any contact between the objects.
> Depth of Knowledge: High
>
> SC.5.P.10.4: Investigate and explain that electrical energy can be transformed into heat, light, and sound energy, as well as the energy of motion.
> Depth of Knowledge: High

Source: Next Generation Sunshine State Standards, *by the Florida Department of Education, 2008.*

Figure 3.5: Florida grade 5 learning standards.

In figure 3.6, the three broad overall expectations for English remain constant for grades 9 and 10. Likewise, the overall expectations for the other strands of the English curriculum remain constant for these two grade levels. Selecting the second of these broad learning targets (speaking to communicate), we find a manageable number of related specific learning targets.

In this jurisdiction, all students must demonstrate proficiency in all three overall expectations for oral communication (listening, speaking, and reflecting), as indeed they must for the overall expectations associated with each of the strands. This requirement is further enforced by requiring teachers to grade and report on student achievement according to these overall expectations. What does this mean for teachers? Consider the city of Toronto, which is home to children from many diverse cultures and backgrounds. Many new Torontonians enter school with very limited facility in either English or French. Despite this, the broad scope of the overall expectations enables teachers to report on the oral communication of all of these students.

Overall Expectations

By the end of this course, students will:

1. Listening to Understand: listen in order to understand and respond appropriately in a variety of situations for a variety of purposes;

2. Speaking to Communicate: use speaking skills and strategies appropriately to communicate with different audiences for a variety of purposes;

3. Reflecting on Skills and Strategies: reflect on and identify their strengths as listeners and speakers, areas for improvement, and the strategies they found most helpful in oral communication and situations.

By the end of this course, students will:

Purpose
2.1 communicate orally for several different purposes, using language suitable for the intended audience

Interpersonal Speaking Strategies
2.2 demonstrate an understanding of several different interpersonal speaking strategies and adapt them to suit the purpose, situation, and audience, exhibiting sensitivity to cultural differences

Clarity and Coherence
2.3 communicate in a clear, coherent manner appropriate to the purpose, subject matter, and intended audience

Diction and Devices
2.4 use appropriate words, phrases, and terminology, and several different stylistic devices, to communicate their meaning and engage their intended audience

Vocal Strategies
2.5 identify several different vocal strategies and use them selectively and with sensitivity to audience needs

Non-Verbal Cues
2.6 identify several different non-verbal cues and use them, with sensitivity to audience needs, to help convey their meaning

Audio-Visual Aids
2.7 use several different audio-visual aids to support and enhance oral presentations

© Queen's Printer for Ontario, 2007. Reproduced with permission.

Figure 3.6: Grade 9 English standards for oral language.

For example, all students are required to "speak to communicate" and to "use speaking skills and strategies appropriately to communicate with different audiences for a variety of purposes." A teacher will differentiate her instruction of speaking skills according to the needs of the new Canadians in her class. Specifically, she will choose from the "specific expectations" listed under "speaking to communicate." For example, for a group of Muslim girls who have recently arrived in Canada from India, she may need to focus instruction on "interpersonal speaking strategies" and "non-verbal cues." Her assessment of the girls' progress will be purely formative, anecdotal, and based on her interactions with them in a combination of small group and one-on-one situations. As individual students improve their skills, the teacher will introduce additional specific expectations from the "speaking to communicate" list.

This is responsive teaching. The same set of broad learning targets must be demonstrated by all students, but the teacher purposefully selects from the specific learning targets in response to the needs that her students present. These needs have been identified and are constantly changing in response to data gathered initially through pre- or diagnostic assessments and updated through ongoing formative assessments.

Essential Learning Versus Coverage of Everything

When teachers focus on a manageable number of broad, essential learning targets for all students, the task of curriculum coverage becomes less daunting. In fact, the focus shifts from curriculum coverage by the teacher to "uncoverage of understanding by students" (Wiggins & McTighe, 1998).

At the beginning of a backward-design unit planning session I was conducting with teachers, I asked each planning team to share with the group the focus of the unit it wished to plan and the reason it had chosen this unit to work on. One team said it wanted to plan a grade 4 science unit on pulleys and gears. When I asked why, one teacher replied, "Because we have to teach this stuff in two weeks, and neither of us understands any of it!" I thanked them for their honesty and asked them to show me the learning outcomes in their science curriculum document. Here is a sampling of those outcomes:

- Describe how rotary motion in one system is transferred to rotary motion in another.

- Describe how gears operate in one plane (for example, spur gears or idler gears) and in two planes (for example, crown, bevel, or worm gears) (Ontario Ministry of Education, 2007b).

I agreed with the grade 4 team that these represented questionable learning targets for nine-year-olds and that, although I was an experienced cyclist and a highly skilled user of gears, if I were to write a test based on knowing these things, I would probably fail miserably! Furthermore, I wouldn't be terribly upset. In other words, I questioned just how essential knowledge of spur, crown, bevel, and worm gears is to students in grade 4. I visit many classes where students have memorized terms and definitions sufficiently well and for just long enough to pass a test, yet have no *understanding*, for example, of the concept of mechanical advantage. Returning to the grade 4 science team, I suggested they begin with essential questions and big ideas to anchor the learning in the pulleys and gears unit. For example:

- Why do we need pulleys and gears? (Essential question)
- They make work easier. (Big idea!)

Later during the workshop, as we worked on matching assessment tasks to curriculum targets, the grade 4 science team quickly realized that a performance task, in which students built either simple pulleys or models of gears, would be necessary to reveal their understanding of mechanical advantage. In this case, the teachers saw that many of the content-based learning outcomes listed in the curriculum were not essential for grade 4 students—outcomes such as "Describe how gears operate in one plane and two planes."

Instead, they recognized that if, by the end of the unit, all students could *demonstrate* their understanding of the big idea—that pulleys and gears make work easier—by building several different pulleys or by riding a bicycle and explaining what was happening as they changed gears, then their teaching would have been successful. Yes, this may necessitate having a bicycle in the classroom! I then described how Rick, a teacher I had recently met, really did have a bicycle mounted on a stationary trainer in his classroom and used it to teach and assess the learning of his students in a variety of subjects, including art, science, and mathematics. He also found the bike to be an excellent anger management tool. Whenever a student began to act out (it was usually a boy), he'd invite him to hop on the bicycle and pedal as fast as he could. Within seconds, the behavior problem transferred into sweat! Yes, this too became a teachable moment about the conservation of energy!

In Rick's classroom, students' energy is focused on essential learning and authentic ways to assess that learning. Furthermore, because he understands the connection between engagement and learning, he is constantly searching for ways to make his teaching and assessment strategies connect with his students' lives and passions.

I worked with another group of grade 4 teachers who were struggling with how to make a unit on light and sound engaging. In the spirit of essential learning, I asked them to consider ways that, on the first day of the unit, they might get their students to appreciate how essential light and sound are in their lives. With some nudging, the team decided to ask their students to briefly experience blindness and deafness using ear plugs and blindfolds. This simulation would lead naturally to a consideration of the importance of protecting one's sight and hearing. Notice, this is simply a hook to engage students at the start of the unit. Depending on the age and grade of students, such a unit may involve more or less theoretical aspects of light and sound, which the teacher would get to eventually. But at the beginning of a new unit of study, it is important to engage students through an activity that will fire connections between a new topic and their own lives.

The key message for teachers when planning is: keep your students clearly in mind as you make decisions about how to introduce learning targets to them. When the curriculum is focused on conceptually complex material, such as the science examples we've been considering, continually ask three questions:

1. What is essential for students to understand?

2. What is essential for students to be able to do?

3. How can I present this material in ways that will engage all of my students?

Conclusion

In today's digital, information-saturated world, educators must engage in debate about the difficult question, what must students learn in school? I emphasize *in school* because so much learning today occurs outside of the classroom. Increasingly, teachers need to be coaches of essential skills, rather than providers of content, because most of what students need to know is at their fingertips on the World Wide Web. Skills, on the other hand, cannot be acquired online. Proficiency in skills requires excellent coaching and constant practice.

A backward design approach to curriculum is not merely desirable, it is essential, because it assists teachers in addressing this question: What must students understand and be able to do as a result of my teaching? Backward design focuses teachers' and students' attention on essential learning—curriculum that is meaningful, relevant, and coherent.

While essential skills and enduring understandings are, by definition, essential and enduring for all students, teachers need to select from the numerous specific learning outcomes appearing in curriculum documents to customize learning to meet the diverse needs of their students. This is challenging but ultimately rewarding work, because it leads, inevitably, to ever-increasing numbers of students meeting with success.

CHAPTER 4

How Should I Assess Students' Needs in the Mixed-Ability Class?

"You have to do DA before you can do DI!" That's my advice to teachers when I introduce the topic of differentiation during a workshop. Whether referred to as diagnostic assessment (DA), preassessment, or initial assessment, teachers must gather data at the start of a year, term, unit, and even at the start of a lesson to determine students' current levels of skill and knowledge, which in turn will enable them to differentiate instruction appropriately. To begin instruction before doing this is, I would argue, tantamount to professional malpractice. How do we know where to begin teaching if we haven't first determined where students are? Why don't more teachers begin the teaching and learning process in this way? In my conversations with teachers, the reasons I most often hear cited are:

- I don't have time.

- I don't have efficient diagnostic assessment tools.

- I wouldn't know what to do with the data I gathered.

- Why do this when I have to cover the same curriculum for everyone anyway?

Yet—based upon my own classroom observations over many years—teachers' failure to begin by gathering preinstructional assessment data is one of the primary reasons students disengage from learning. When curriculum and instruction are not tailored to the needs of students, some find learning too challenging, while others find it boring. In either case, the consequences are often similar: disengagement, truancy, failure to complete assigned work, and inappropriate behavior. Lev Vygotsky (1978) and Mihaly Csikszentmihalyi (1990) both point to the need to target instruction and assessment at levels that maximize learning. Vygotsky defined this level as the "zone of proximal development," which challenges but does not frustrate the learner (Vygotsky, 1978). The zone of proximal development

> is the distance between the actual developmental level as determined by independent problem solving and the level of potential development as determined through problem solving under adult guidance or in collaboration with more capable peers. . . . what is in the zone of proximal development today will be the actual developmental level tomorrow—that is, what a child can do with assistance today she will be able to do by herself tomorrow. (pp. 86–87)

Vygotsky's comments identify the importance of the teacher adjusting the amount of support provided to the learner, with autonomy being the goal.

In an interview, Csikszentmihalyi described as "flow" the common quality of experience of people who felt that what they were doing was going really well. This experience, he found, was characterized by the fact that

> you were completely immersed in what you were doing, that the concentration was very high, that you knew what you had to do moment by moment, that you had very quick and precise feedback as to how well you were doing, and that you felt that your abilities were stretched but not overwhelmed by the opportunities for action. In other words, the challenges were in balance with the skills. And when those conditions were present, you began to forget all the things that bothered you in everyday life, forget the self as an entity separate from what was going on—you felt you were a part of something greater and you were just moving along with the logic of the activity.
>
> Everyone said that it was like being carried by a current, spontaneous, effortless like a flow. (Debold, 2002)

The concepts of zone of proximal development and flow, as they apply to education, tell us that students learn best when they perceive a task as being achievable and when they are required to think and persevere in the face of challenge.

It is a serious misconception to believe that students, especially those with learning difficulties, like work that is easy. Observe a child or adolescent with a new videogame. Upon first booting it up, he may be stumped by it. But then his innate ability to problem solve kicks into high gear! He may simply begin playing the game and learn through trial and error, while at the same time collaborating with friends on his iPhone or Facebook. Whatever the learning strategy, within minutes, the gamer is playing at the highest challenge level.

Young people enjoy challenges; they thrive on them; they are effective problem solvers—but only when they are engaged and see what they are doing as worthwhile.

But as a teacher said to me recently when I made this observation at a recent workshop, "Sure, but those games are engaging. School's not like that."

"Perhaps it needs to be," I suggested. "Perhaps we need to ensure that the tasks we set for students are innately engaging." Such tasks—like video-games—need to involve simulation, role playing, and decision making in ever more complex situations, as well as make use of instructional technology.

To ensure that students are working within their zone of proximal development, to increase the likelihood that they will experience a state of flow, and to maximize engagement, teachers must take the time to conduct diagnostic or preassessment, especially at the beginning of the year, term, or semester. Diagnostic assessment plays a vital role in planning for the mixed-ability class and provides teachers with the information necessary to adjust curriculum and instruction to best address learning needs.

On What Basis Should Teachers Differentiate Instruction?

Tomlinson (2001) identifies three variables that need to be examined when making decisions about differentiation:

1. **Readiness to learn**—a student's entry point relative to a particular understanding or skill

2. **Interest**—child's affinity, curiosity, or passion for a particular topic or skill

3. **Learning profile**—how students learn best, including information such as multiple intelligences (MI), learning styles, and learning barriers and aptitudes

Determining Students' Readiness to Learn

I recently visited Carolyn's grade 2 class and was struck by the on-task behavior of all her students. More specifically, I observed that:

- All students were enthusiastically engaged in their work.
- Students were well behaved and respectful of each other.

- Students were resourceful, relying upon each other for support.

- Carolyn moved easily and efficiently from group to group, providing direction and assistance as required.

- The different materials being used at the various stations around the room reflected thorough planning and preparation to meet a variety of needs.

During my chat with Carolyn at the end of the day, I asked, "What kinds of data do you use in order to provide such a range of students with materials that are targeted at their instructional levels?"

Carolyn then shared her process with me (fig. 4.1).

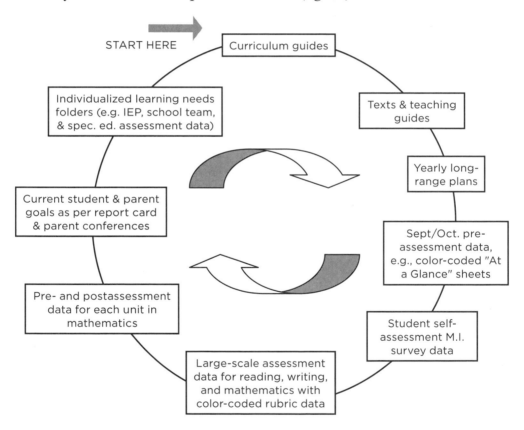

Source: Personal communication, Carolyn Williamson, June 30, 2010. Used with permission.

Figure 4.1: Carolyn's data for informing differentiation in her grade 2 class.

She begins her planning for differentiation in early September by reviewing the curriculum guides, texts, and teaching guides for her assigned grade and then reviews preestablished annual long-range plans. Once her students are comfortably settled into the new school year, she conducts a variety of preassessments to gather data about students' prior knowledge, skills, interests, and learning preferences. As the fall term progresses, Carolyn gathers what she calls "large-scale assessment data" using commercial tools such as *PM Benchmarks* (Nelley & Smith, 2001). At the beginning and end of each unit in mathematics, Carolyn administers pre- and postassessments. The first reporting period and subsequent parent conferences are key points in the formative assessment process, because they enable Carolyn to supplement her own data with information that parents provide. Throughout this cycle, to meet the needs of certain of her students, Carolyn collaborates with the school team and special education resource teacher to set goals, monitor progress, and provide interventions as necessary. This enables her to choose the most appropriate texts and lesson plans based on the most current needs and learning styles of her class.

The cyclical nature of Carolyn's process reflects the dynamic nature of her teaching. She is constantly gathering further data about her students to ensure that her teaching is responsive to their ever-changing needs.

Damian's Grade 9 English Class

In my own teaching career, I relied upon a combination of experience and instinct to ensure that my instruction was responsive to the needs of all students. Here, for example, is a summary of the preassessment strategies I employed to gather baseline data about the writing skills of students in a grade 9 English class of students enrolled in a vocational program.

Using Spandel's six writing traits (Spandel, 2002) as an organizer, I began gathering diagnostic data on students' writing on the first day of the term by leading them through a guided visualization about how they saw themselves ten years in the future. I asked them to visualize their homes, their families, their workplace, and their leisure time, and then to write down everything they saw and heard on their journey. At this point, I did not allow students to word process, nor did I offer to scribe for anyone. I needed a sample of their independent writing skills, produced without any aids or support. During the next few days, I gathered several more samples of their writing, including responses to a newspaper article, a video, a creative writing prompt, and a response to a personal letter that I wrote to the class. By examining their writing in all of these modes—descriptive, expository, creative, and personal—I was able to build a profile of each student's strengths and needs with respect to the six traits.

I also used a personal interest survey, coupled with brief one-on-one interviews to discover each student's out-of-school interests and passions. Sure enough, some students' initial response to my question, "What do you really care about or love to do?" was "Nuthin,'" but I would not accept this as an answer. My message to teachers is, "Don't give up on anyone! Don't let any student opt out of learning."

Needless to say, the quality of writing from all students reflected a wide range of skills. My next task was to form manageable instructional groups, based on the data I had gathered. A portion of the data appears in figure 4.2. In the interests of space, the table includes only some of my students.

Skill Deficits (Numbers represent priority of each trait. 1 = highest; 6 = lowest)						
Groups	Ideas	Organiza-tion	Voice	Word Choice	Sentence Fluency	Conven-tions
Tannis	1	2	6	5	4	3
George	2	1	6	5	4	3
Su Tan	1	2	5	6	4	3
Grant	1	2	6	5	4	3
Ricky			4	3	1	2
Elise			3	4	2	1
Mandip			3	4	2	1
Ellis			4	3	2	1

Figure 4.2: A sample of write traits diagnostic data.

The numbers represent the priority with which I needed to address students' needs. For example, Tannis, George, Su Tan, and Grant had more serious skill deficits than Ricky, Elise, Mandip, and Ellis. The data analysis enabled me to organize the following instructional groups:

1. Ideas—Tannis, Su Tan, Grant

2. Conventions—Elise, Mandip, Ellis

3. Sentence fluency—Ricky

4. Organization—George

I then prepared mini lessons—ten to fifteen minutes in length, occurring within the lesson as a whole—to address the priority trait of each group. A typical lesson looked like this:

1. Begin with a confirmation of the skill deficit by examining students' work. I sit with students in a circle, and we read several work samples and highlight a specific problem: for example, the main idea in the expository piece is not clear.

2. Teach the skill, and check orally for understanding. We read an exemplary piece in which the main idea is clear. I facilitate discussion in which I assess students' ability to explain the strength of the exemplar. We then review the problem in the student sample, and I invite suggestions for improving it. Can they correct it?

3. Those students who are able to correct the error then work in pairs to correct similar errors on other work samples.

4. I continue to work with those students who continue to have difficulty with the concept of main idea. I provide practice, orally, identifying and correcting the error.

5. I continue monitoring the work of the pairs and encourage them to share their revisions with other pairs.

6. Once students' practice work in pairs indicates mastery of the skill, they work independently on their own original piece of work to correct the problem.

Daily mini lessons like this provide specific instruction to groups of students demonstrating similar problems. Note, however, that for such lessons to be productive, the rest of the class must be engaged in meaningful work, with a clear understanding of the behavioral norms that were established at the beginning of the term. Before a mini lesson occurs, I take the time to review with the class the T-chart that highlights what independent work looks and sounds like (see page 66).

Finally, the different groups of students were assigned different writing tasks, each designed to provide opportunities to improve their targeted skill. As students demonstrated mastery of a particular trait, they moved on to their next area of need. For example, once Tannis, Su Tan, and Grant were able to infuse their writing with more original ideas, they began to focus on their second priority: organization.

Determining Students' Interests

Teachers need to determine students' interests so that they can adapt materials and tasks in order to engage them more deeply in learning.

Consider Carlos, who, despite all of my efforts, refused to engage with learning in my class—until the day I discovered that soccer was his passion. Because I was far more concerned with improving Carlos' reading, writing, and speaking skills than I was with having him master any specific content, I permitted him to read, write, and speak about soccer! Because this was the one area in which he had interest and ability, he was willing to deal with texts far beyond his instructional reading level and to persevere in decoding unfamiliar words and comprehending complex sentence structures that would have caused him to shut down had he encountered them in required texts. Were I teaching Carlos today, online access to match reports about his favorite team, Benfica, would be at our fingertips, presenting numerous opportunities to enrich Carlos' reading or writing skills.

In my actual classroom experience with Carlos, once he gained confidence and demonstrated some command over reading and writing skills, I began to introduce some of the required course materials. This is a fundamental principle of differentiation: if improving literacy skills is the goal, teachers must make available to students materials that are most likely to engage their interest.

While there is no shortage of tools for determining students' interests, there is no substitute for teachers' use of their ears, eyes, and relationship-building skills to determine what each student most cares about. This requires that teachers continually observe and listen to students as they interact with their peers, both in class and elsewhere in the school. Pay attention to clubs and activities in which they enroll; note what they choose to read when there are no limits placed upon them. In middle and high schools, talk to the rest of their teachers or to teachers from previous grades. And of course, talk to their parents.

Engaged students learn; disengaged students don't!

Determining Students' Learning Profiles

Tomlinson (2001) identifies four broad categories for teachers to consider when determining students' learning profiles (fig. 4.3).

Group Orientation	Learning Environment
independent/self-orientation	quiet/noise
group/peer orientation	warm/cool
adult orientation	still/mobile
combination	flexible/fixed
	"busy"/"spare"
Cognitive Style	**Intelligence Preference**
creative/conforming	analytic
essence/facts	practical
whole-to-part/part-to-whole	creative
expressive/controlled	verbal/linguistic
nonlinear/linear	logical/mathematical
inductive/deductive	spatial/visual
people-oriented/task- or object-oriented	bodily/kinesthetic
concrete/abstract	musical/rhythmic
collaboration/competition	interpersonal
interpersonal/introspective	intrapersonal
easily distracted/long attention span	naturalist
group achievement/personal achievement	existential
oral/visual/kinesthetic	
reflective/action-oriented	

Source: Carol Ann Tomlinson, How to Differentiate Instruction in Mixed-Ability Classrooms, *2nd ed. Alexandria, VA: ASCD. © 2001 by ASCD. Reprinted with permission. Learn more about ASCD at www.ascd.org.*

Figure 4.3: Tomlinson's learning profile factors.

The specific dimensions within each of the four categories reflect the frameworks of a number of highly respected educational researchers and theorists, including Howard Gardner *(Frames of Mind: The Theory of Multiple Intelligences,* 1983). Robert Sternberg *(Beyond IQ: A Triarchic Theory of Human Intelligence,* 1985), and Bernice McCarthy *(About Learning,* 1996), developer of 4-MAT.

For inexperienced teachers as well as those who are struggling with the demands of mixed-ability classrooms, the myriad variables listed in figure 4.3 can be intimidating. However, figure 4.4 (page 52) may help to clarify the focus for the four categories, as well as strategies for gathering data about each one.

While learning profile frameworks are useful for helping teachers understand the many variables they need to consider when program planning, they are sometimes used as a substitute for the timeless professional skills of observing and listening to students engaged in the learning process. In my experience, multiple intelligences tools are among those most commonly used in superficial and inappropriate ways.

Category	Focus of Category	Strategies for Assessing Students' Preferences	Teacher Actions
Group Orientation	Degree to which students prefer to work independently or with others Degree to which students relate better to peers or to adults	Observation of behaviors One-on-one interview Discussion with school resource team Discussion with parents	Have students work independently, with a peer, in groups, with you, or in the optimum combination of these.
Cognitive Style	How students think How students learn	Learning styles and multiple intelligences inventories Observation of behaviors One-on-one interview Assessment of work samples Examination of student records	Differentiate your instruction and the work students complete to ensure they are challenged appropriately.
Learning Environment	How students experience their environment through their senses	Observation of behaviors One-on-one interview	Adjust environmental conditions to maximize learning.
Intelligence Preference	How a student interacts with people, places, things, and situations	Learning styles and multiple intelligences inventories Observation of behaviors One-on-one interview Assessment of work samples	Differentiate your instruction and the work students complete to ensure they are challenged appropriately.

Figure 4.4: Gathering data to prepare student learning profiles.

In March 1997, I was in the audience as Howard Gardner delivered a keynote address at the annual Association for Supervision and Curriculum Development (ASCD) conference. He spoke with great sadness about the frequent misunderstanding and misapplication of his work in multiple intelligences. In particular, he regretted the use of simplistic tools to quickly determine the intelligence profile of a class and then allowing students to work in their "strongest intelligence" whenever tasks were assigned. The consequences of such an approach to differentiation can include students working far below their abilities and making little, if any, progress in those skills where they have deficits. Furthermore, marks and grades derived from a smorgasbord of choices frequently have little connection to essential learning goals or curriculum targets. Such superficial applications of MI are certainly unworthy of the tag *research based*. And, unfortunately, superficial application of MI principles and strategies may occur for no other reason than teachers being required to comply with school or district-level improvement plans.

Because the scientific community remains skeptical of the validity of MI, its inappropriate application should be of particular concern to all educators. Reporting on the widespread influence of MI, journalist James Traub wrote:

> In the 15 years since the publication of Gardner's *Frames of Mind*, multiple intelligences has gone from being a widely disputed theory to a rallying cry for school reformers to a cultural commonplace. And, amazingly, it has done so without ever winning over the scientific establishment. (Traub, 1998, p. 21)

My point in raising these concerns is simply that effective differentiated practice requires a great deal more than a single MI survey. As with all assessment, valid conclusions may be drawn only once multiple sources of data have been gathered at different times and in different contexts, and the data from these assessments have been analyzed by careful, thoughtful professionals. Data-*less* decisions are bad decisions, just as are data-*driven* decisions. Sound decisions are data *informed* and blend data analysis with a teacher's professional judgment and intuition.

All decisions that teachers make regarding differentiating instruction and assessment must be both purposeful and strategic—purposeful in the sense that they should optimize learning for every student, and strategic in the sense that they are essential to realizing that purpose. Conversely, there are times when it may not be necessary or desirable to differentiate at all. A field trip to a local marsh to learn about the importance of wetlands to the environment may well suit *all* students' interests and learning preferences. Differentiation may not occur until everyone is back in the classroom, when it may be necessary to differentiate follow-up tasks to assess students' learning.

Similarly, in a welding class, while the teacher may find it necessary to differentiate her instructional approach to ensure that all students understand how to maximize the strength of the joints they are going to weld, the performance assessment task and related performance standards must remain the same for all students. Why? Because all welds must meet industrial standards and must be assessed on a pass/fail basis (see chapter 9).

Conclusion

Teachers cannot do DI until they've done DA. In other words, effective differentiation can occur only when teachers have conducted thorough pre- or diagnostic assessment at the beginning of a term, semester, unit, or even lesson. Such assessment enables the teacher to determine each student's zone of proximal development and to establish a manageable number of instructional groupings to maximize learning for all students.

Pre- or diagnostic assessment must serve primarily to determine students' readiness to learn. Specifically, this involves identifying gaps in prerequisite knowledge and skills. Preassessment also identifies students' interests, as well as their learning preferences. The latter include grouping preferences, cognitive styles, environmental preferences, and multiple intelligences preferences.

The purpose of gathering all of this information is to tailor instruction and assessment to optimize learning for all. This requires the strategic, purposeful matching of resources, instructional strategies, grouping configurations, environmental variables, and formative assessment methods to students' profiles.

CHAPTER 5

What Does Excellence Look Like in the Mixed-Ability Class?

The differentiated classroom is, by definition, a responsive classroom—responsive in the sense that the teacher looks at the class not as a whole but as an assembly of unique individuals, each with certain learning needs, preferences, and interests. For many teachers, particularly those teaching in the middle and high school grades, this represents a considerable challenge, faced as they are with an imposing curriculum to cover. But as we have seen, curriculum coverage by the teacher does not necessarily equate to learning on the part of students. Furthermore, the Internet has placed knowledge at the fingertips of students. Teachers are no longer students' primary source of knowledge—if indeed they ever were! Increasingly, the role of the teacher in the 21st century is to facilitate the integration of essential concepts with the essential skills that students need in order to navigate the digital world in which they live—skills such as critical thinking and problem solving.

Two factors contribute to the tension that teachers experience as they struggle to meet the changing and diverse needs of today's students: lack of training and, as Grant Wiggins (1994a) has pointed out, a confusion of "standards," which are necessary and desirable, with "standardization," which is neither!

Teacher Training

The education and training that most teachers have received has focused upon mastery of content knowledge in a specific discipline. Most of us are qualified experts in one or more subject areas, but we have not been trained to diagnose and remediate the skill deficits exhibited by today's typical mixed-ability class. Those teachers who have trained as early childhood specialists are a notable exception. They may have received extensive training in the assessment and instruction of the sets of basic skills that comprise much of the curriculum in kindergarten to grade 2. Many teachers I meet in the junior division (grades 3–6) are also highly skilled in diagnosing the diverse learning needs of their students, as well as differentiating instruction to address these needs.

But most teachers with whom I work in the middle and high school grades readily admit that their training did *not* prepare them for the demands they face daily with their students. We (yes, I am one of these teachers!) were trained as content specialists, not as skills coaches. I use this analogy quite purposefully. The sports team coach must be able to work with a diverse group of individuals, first of all assessing their current skill levels, and then drawing upon a vast repertoire of strategies and tools to improve the skills of each player. Effective coaches rely upon observation, monitoring, strategy selection, adjusting on the fly, and making ongoing adjustment of interventions, to name but a few of the skills they must employ. Furthermore, the successful coach is attuned to the emotional, attitudinal, and behavioral proclivities of the athletes in his or her charge. So, while having knowledge of the rules of the game and the strengths and weaknesses of other teams is necessary, the coach's greatest assets are his or her *skills,* because those skills are necessary to enable each athlete to achieve his or her potential.

The training of the typical teacher involves memorization of vast amounts of factual information—in subject areas that may or may not be relevant to that teacher's eventual teaching assignments—usually with the goal of passing examinations. Once a teacher is employed in a school, his or her role quite naturally shifts from *recipient* of knowledge to *transmitter* of knowledge. And as long as the classroom is viewed as a homogeneous collection of students, the teacher's primary responsibility is to cover the curriculum once, in the same way, for everyone. Assessment, then, ensures that students are sorted into high, average, and low achievers, based on their ability to demonstrate knowledge on tests.

However, as we saw in chapter 1 (page 7), today's focus on meeting the needs of all learners has called this paradigm into question. Educational leaders at both the district and school levels are now expecting teachers to adjust what they teach, how they teach, and how they assess in order to meet the differing needs of all students in the class. Regrettably, few teachers I meet have been trained in the skills and strategies to do this. The result? Frustration for teachers and insufficient learning for many students.

The Standards Movement

Another obstacle to flexible, responsive teaching is a consequence of the standards movement. In the 1980s, the educational community turned to industry in its quest for school improvement models. Much of the impetus for the standards movement in education was influenced by industry's focus on output rather than input as a measure of quality. This resulted in a shift away from measuring success according to whether a teacher had covered curriculum objectives toward measuring success according to student results. While this emphasis on output indicators has led to much positive change, there are dangers inherent in applying industrial improvement models to education. Greatest among these is adopting a one-size-fits-all approach to curriculum and instruction. Industries are successful when they engage in research and development to create a high-quality product—a car, a computer, a mobile phone—and then employ quality-control mechanisms to produce thousands of identical copies of that product. Thus, in industry, quality is defined in terms of sameness of output. Schools, by contrast, have a responsibility to uncover and nurture the individual potential of all of their students. Sameness should be seen as anathema to high-quality education.

As the standards movement has evolved, excellence has emerged as a popular rallying cry, among both educational leaders and politicians. But excellence in the educational context requires a different set of indicators than it does in industry. Too many educational leaders equate the pursuit of excellence with raising test scores or increasing the number of students demonstrating proficiency on the same set of narrow learning outcomes. "Our goal in this district is to raise test scores!" How often have I heard politicians and senior administrators stand proudly before an audience to announce this as their mission. I can barely contain my rage when I hear this message delivered publicly to teachers and parents. Achieving excellence, when defined this way, leads to endless drill and practice and to the development in students of "test-wiseness" rather than learning and understanding. According to assessment expert Dylan Wiliam:

> The trouble with such "objective" approaches is that while many things can be measured, there are also many important things that cannot, and the danger is that the things that can be measured easily come to be regarded as more important than those that cannot. . . . We start out with the aim of making the important measurable, and end up making only the measurable important. . . .

If you make a particular performance indicator a policy target, and make the stakes high enough, then the people at the sharp end will do everything they can to improve the score on the performance indicator. However, because the areas in which we use performance indicators are so complex, there is always a way of improving the performance indicator without having any impact on the overall quality of whatever the performance indicator is meant to be measuring. (Wiliam, 2001)

My home province in Canada provides a disturbing example of the risks inherent in politically driven standard setting. In Ontario, the Student Success/Learning to 18 strategy set as one of its targets increasing secondary-school graduation rates from 68 percent in 2003–04 to 85 percent by 2010–11, surely a laudable goal. And as figure 5.1 indicates, the strategy appears destined to achieve this goal.

Year	Graduation Rate	Total Graduates[1]	Additional Graduates since 2003/2004
2003/2004	68%	102,000	—
2004/2005	71%	106,500	4,500
2005/2006	73%	109,500	7,500
2006/2007	75%	112,400	10,500
Total		430,500	22,500

[1]Approximate numbers

© *Queen's Printer for Ontario, 2010. Reproduced with permission.*

Figure 5.1: Provincial graduation rates, Ontario Ministry of Education.

Unfortunately, one of the consequences of this top-down, political pressure tactic is that teachers are feeling compelled to pass students who have not demonstrated proficiency. Teachers have expressed this concern to me countless times during workshops. Figure 5.2 serves to confirm this serious issue.

So what constitutes excellence in education? How should we define it? What indicators should we use to measure it? And once we have defined it, how do we promote it among teachers, students, and parents?

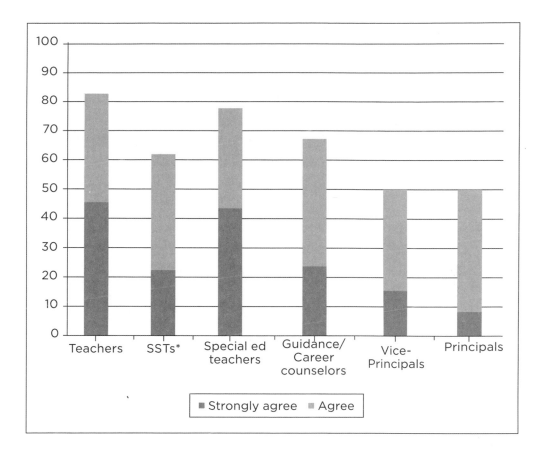

SST = Student Success Teachers.

Source: Evaluation of the Ontario Ministry of Education's Student Success/Learning to 18 Strategy: Final Report *(p. 59), by C. Ungerleider, 2008, Ottawa, ON, Canada: Canadian Council on Learning. Reprinted with permission.*

Figure 5.2: Do educators believe that schools are under too much pressure to improve graduation and pass rates?

Defining Excellence

The goal for schools and school districts must be to maximize learning for all students. Large-scale standardized test scores are only one of many measures that may be used to assess the quality of learning demonstrated by students. Most large-scale standardized tests assess a relatively narrow band of knowledge outcomes. They typically provide little or no evidence of understanding, of the application of knowledge to unfamiliar situations, or of skill demonstration beyond memorization.

So, if test scores alone are not indicators of excellence, what are? Wiggins and McTighe (1998) have suggested that worthwhile educational outcomes must be measured in terms of understanding, not merely knowledge. They conceptualize student understanding in terms of the following six facets:

1. Explanation—sophisticated and apt explanations and theories that provide knowledgeable and justified accounts of events, actions, and ideas

2. Interpretation—interpretations, narratives, and translations that provide meaning

3. Application—ability to use knowledge effectively in new situations and diverse contexts

4. Perspective—critical and insightful points of view

5. Empathy—the ability to get inside another person's feelings and worldview

6. Self-knowledge—the wisdom to know one's ignorance and how one's patterns of thought and action inform as well as prejudice understanding

(Wiggins & McTighe, 1998, pp. 45–57)

Clearly, if understanding is as complex as this framework suggests, valid assessment demands a much richer and more diverse set of strategies and tools than mere tests of content.

Highly skilled teachers—those proficient in differentiating instruction and assessment—understand the limitations of standardized tests and do their best to gather a more balanced sample of evidence of student learning. These samples include portfolios, student-designed products, performances, and increasingly, digital products such as web pages, wikis, and blogs. Assessment-literate teachers know how to design assessments that will enable them to collect a wide range of evidence of learning; they also know how to analyze data from these assessments in order to draw valid conclusions about their students' knowledge, understanding, and skills.

In my own work, I frequently see remarkable demonstrations of excellent learning, and inevitably these examples involve students synthesizing knowledge and skills and applying a unique combination of them in challenging, authentic contexts. These demonstrations include students rehearsing and presenting professional-quality dramas and musicals they have written; video footage of students building a house in Africa and a school in Venezuela; blueprints and models of interior designs that students subsequently installed for local businesses; food school, baking, and restaurant services' students catering and serving food at school open houses, arts fests, and "excellence evenings." In classrooms, I have seen students so immersed in simulations that they respond to questions in role as they explain how they are negotiating with their G8 counterparts at an economic summit or representing the United States at an environmental conference about climate change.

Clearly, excellence in learning and achievement must be defined far more broadly than high scores on standardized tests of knowledge! On a recent overseas trip, I picked up a business magazine. The cover story related to the selection of candidates for business schools, as well as the curriculum currently delivered at those schools. After I read the articles relating to the cover story, it was clear that:

- Current college selection procedures, which rely almost exclusively on examination results, are not identifying potentially successful candidates for the business world of the 21st century.

- Current course offerings in the country's business schools are preparing students for yesterday's business reality.

A second indicator of excellence begs the question, excellence for whom? When speaking about districtwide targets, senior educational leaders often speak of the need to raise the bar. The metaphor has great appeal, because few would argue with schools committing themselves to improving student achievement. But extending the metaphor, we must ask ourselves how excellence should be measured with respect to achievement. Should it be measured:

- In terms of how high the highest jumpers are able to soar?

- In terms of how many jumpers clear the bar at a minimally acceptable level?

- According to the narrowing of the gap between the highest and lowest jumpers?

- On all three of these dimensions?

Clearly, when schools and districts embrace differentiated instruction, they are committing to all three measures of excellence. In the words of Rick DuFour and his colleagues, our mission as educators must be *Raising the Bar and Closing the Gap* (DuFour, DuFour, Eaker, & Karhanek, 2010).

Creating the Conditions for Excellence to Thrive

In order to create conditions for excellence to thrive in our schools, teachers need to focus on four elements: classroom climate, program planning, understanding the relationship between assessment *for* and assessment *of* learning, and quality work.

Classroom Climate

Highly effective classrooms are those in which time on-task is maximized and, as a result, the learning of all students is optimized. Some years ago, I attended the twenty-five year reunion of a school where I had taught. A young man approached and said, "Mr. Cooper, do you remember me?" While the face was vaguely familiar, I couldn't summon a name from memory.

"I'm Des. You taught me and my brother. And we were bad!"

Then, sure enough, the memories flooded back. Des and his younger brother had almost driven me to distraction through their behavior!

Des continued, "I came here tonight to say thanks. I now own my own trucking rig; I'm married with two kids. Life's good. But if it hadn't been for you, I would have dropped out of school. Even though I was a bad kid, you didn't give up on me. And you were always firm but fair."

Creating a classroom climate that is firm but fair strikes the best possible balance of structure and flexibility. Structures need to be in place to ensure that essential curriculum is addressed and that learning occurs; flexibility ensures that the teacher adjusts conditions to suit the needs of all students. Of course, the foundation on which the classroom climate must rest is the relationship between teacher and students. Here are some suggestions for establishing a firm but fair classroom climate in which the goal is optimizing learning for all students:

- Establish norms by which you and your students will work together.
- Establish clear expectations and consequences for work habits and behavior.
- Conduct frequent monitoring to ensure that these expectations are met by all.

Establish Norms

Within minutes of arriving in a classroom, I can determine whether or not time has been spent establishing norms by which the teacher and students will interact. In learning environments where norms are in place, I typically witness the following:

- Expectations for behavior are clearly displayed.

- Students are on task most or all of the time.

- The teacher takes a few moments before a task begins to highlight the learning goal for the lesson, as well as the social skill or behavior associated with the task.

- Students speak respectfully to each other and to the teacher.

- Students see their peers as resources just as much as their teacher.

- Discipline is applied by the teacher quietly, unobtrusively, privately, fairly, and appropriately relative to the misdemeanor.

- Interactions are positive, supportive, and good-humored.

- Contributions are sought from all students and all contributions are valued.

In learning environments where norms are either absent or not enforced, simply add the word *not* to each of these indicators!

What does a set of learning environment norms look like, and how should they be identified? Figure 5.3 shows Rachel's norms for her grade 8 social studies class.

Norms for Students

At all times:
- Arrive on time.
- Show respect for self and others.
- Do your best on all tasks.
- Seek help from peers (three before me—teacher).
- Inform me about problems that might interfere with your work.

Norms for Ms. Taylor

- Treat us all fairly.
- Return work promptly.
- Listen to our concerns.
- No tests on Friday.
- Make jokes!

Figure 5.3: Norms of behavior in a grade 8 classroom.

How did Rachel establish these norms for her classroom? In a word, *collaboratively.* On the first day of the term, she engaged her students in a discussion about the connections among behaviors, social relationships, and success in school. The culmination of this discussion was an invitation to students to create a set of their expectations for her, in return for accepting her expectations for them.

The reason I remain so positive and passionate about my work as a consultant is that I constantly discover learning environments in which learning is maximized, discipline problems are rare, students are engaged, and teachers are fulfilled. What characterizes these situations?

- **The quality of teacher-student relationships**—The teacher and students interact respectfully, *all the time*. The teacher addresses students by name, thanks them for contributions, and praises them when work is deserving of praise. The teacher acknowledges that children and adolescents make poor decisions, and so constantly reminds them of her expectations—and does this *before* work begins, setting up students for success, not failure. Humor is used frequently to enhance the learning climate. But the teacher does *not* try to endear herself to students by dressing, speaking, or behaving as they do. A line of respect clearly delineates teacher from students.

- **The relevance and authenticity of the work being done**— Students do their best on assigned work because they see the work as worth doing. They may have had input into the nature of the task; time may have been spent establishing a connection between the task and the world beyond school; students' questions about the relevance of the task may have been discussed openly and honestly; and the teacher may have explained how this smaller task connects to a major summative task.

- **The use of technology to enhance the learning experience**— Today's students are "digital natives," and depending on their age, many teachers are "digital immigrants" (Prensky, 2001). Information technologies, by their very nature and design, engage students as active participants in learning. When using instructional technology appropriately, students have to think and make decisions, and consequently, they learn.

Establish Clear Expectations and Consequences

While many teachers admit to spending time on the first day of a new term establishing norms with their students, many struggle to adhere to those norms as the year unfolds. For norms to have an ongoing impact on learning and productivity, they must be highlighted daily. Here's what this looks like in Courtney's grade 3 class.

Courtney's Grade 3 Class

Courtney has a rambunctious group of third graders. To help her students focus their thinking and energy, she clearly identifies both an academic and a social goal for each lesson. The academic goals derive from her grade 3 curriculum documents; the social goals derive from the set of six learning skills and work habits that she is expected to teach, assess, and report on (fig. 5.4).

Responsibility	Organization
• Fulfills responsibilities and commitments within the learning environment • Completes and submits class work, homework, and assignments according to agreed-upon timelines • Takes responsibility for and manages own behavior	• Devises and follows a plan and process for completing work and tasks • Establishes priorities and manages time to complete tasks and achieve goals • Identifies, gathers, evaluates, and uses information, technology, and resources to complete tasks
Independent Work	**Collaboration**
• Independently monitors, assesses, and revises plans to complete tasks and meet goals • Uses class time appropriately to complete tasks • Follows instructions with minimal supervision	• Accepts various roles and an equitable share of work in a group • Responds positively to the ideas, opinions, values, and traditions of others • Builds healthy peer-to-peer relationships through personal and media-assisted interactions • Works with others to resolve conflicts and build consensus to achieve group goals • Shares information, resources, and expertise, and promotes critical thinking to solve problems and make decisions
Initiative	**Self-Regulation**
• Looks for and acts on new ideas and opportunities for learning • Demonstrates the capacity for innovation and a willingness to take risks • Demonstrates curiosity and interest in learning • Approaches new tasks with a positive attitude • Recognizes and advocates appropriately for the rights of self and others	• Sets own individual goals, and monitors progress toward achieving them • Seeks clarification or assistance when needed • Assesses and reflects critically on own strengths, needs, and interests • Identifies learning opportunities, choices, and strategies to meet personal needs and achieve goals • Perseveres and makes an effort when responding to challenges

© Queen's Printer for Ontario, 2010. Reproduced with permission.

Figure 5.4: Learning skills and work habits.

In the early weeks of the fall term, as the need to focus on one of these skills occurs for the first time, Courtney engages her students in a concept attainment lesson, in which they identify the indicators for the specific skill. The result of the lesson is a "looks like . . . sounds like . . ." T-chart that is used throughout the year whenever this learning skill is important to the success of the lesson (fig. 5.5). Through this combination of clear learning goals (both achievement and behavioral), collaboratively developed behavioral norms that are public and constantly reinforced, and the gradual transfer of responsibility for enforcing the norms from teacher to student, Courtney is able to train her students to monitor and adjust their own behaviors.

Initiative	
Looks Like	Sounds Like
· Solving problems myself	· Quiet talk with classmates
· Three before me	· Self-talk
· Going to the word wall	

Figure 5.5: Student-teacher developed T-chart for initiative.

Conduct Frequent Monitoring

One of the most significant educational research finding of the past decade has been the impact of formative assessment or assessment *for* learning on improving student learning (Black, Harrison, Lee, Marshall, & Wiliam, 2004). Applying this research to classroom climate, frequent, ongoing assessment of the social interactions and behaviors in the learning environment is essential to maximize learning. I first discovered this when teaching in a composite high school in the early 1980s. Faced with behaviors and attitudes that placed student learning (and my own sanity!) at risk, I instituted Friday meetings to gather data about the implementation of the norms in each of my classes. The agenda was simple. Each Friday, we asked three questions of ourselves as a learning community:

1. What did we do well this week?

2. What didn't we do well this week?

3. What do we need to do differently next week?

I would facilitate the meeting early in the semester, but once my students understood the procedure, I handed responsibility to them. Norms ensured that the meeting did not become personal. For example, students would not mention their peers by name when identifying problems. Points recorded in response to the third question—what do we need to do differently?—were captured on chart paper and posted. These became the focal point for monitoring improvement during the following week, thereby ensuring that the students learned from their past experiences and were constantly striving to improve the learning climate.

Program Planning

So many teachers say, "How do I manage my high school classes if I have students moving at different speeds? I have so much to cover!" or "How can I insist on all of my students mastering essential learning? At the end of a unit, we have to move on!"

I've heard these questions too many times to count! "Covering all of the curriculum outcomes" required by the curriculum has become an increasingly difficult challenge for teachers, especially in the middle and high school grades, as standards-based curricula have become the norm across the United States and Canada. This challenge is seen as being insurmountable by teachers who are told that excellence from all is the new mission of schools. In other words, if the new mission of schools is to ensure that *all* students leave a given grade or course having mastered essential understandings and skills, it follows that many students will need to resubmit work and rewrite tests and assignments until they meet the required criteria. With the ever-widening range of prerequisite knowledge and skills exhibited in a given class today, it's not surprising that teachers are daunted by their task.

How can this dilemma be addressed?

1. Collaborate with your grade or course colleagues in identifying essential learning.

2. Admit that a large proportion of what we expect students to learn will be forgotten as soon as the unit is over.

3. Recognize that students will learn far more during their educational careers from sources other than their teachers.

4. Understand that students are capable problem solvers and are able to learn independently of teachers and other adults when they are motivated to learn, are engaged with learning, and see what they are doing as relevant, meaningful, and worth doing.

5. Acknowledge that, when empowered, students become highly effective resources for each other and, consequently, become less dependent on their teacher as the primary source of learning.

By examining and discussing curriculum documents collaboratively with colleagues, teachers can quickly become experts at planning their programs and units in ways that maximize learning for all students (see chapter 3, page 31).

Understanding the Relationship Between Assessment for and Assessment of Learning

When I ask participants in a workshop, "How many of you are familiar with the terms *assessment* for *learning* and *assessment* of *learning?*" (Stiggins et al., 2004), the majority of hands go up. But awareness of terms does not necessarily translate into effective implementation in the learning environment.

While *assessment* for *learning* is frequently used synonymously with *formative assessment,* all too often formative assessment is simply "summative lite." In other words, formative assessment is often just another opportunity to assign scores to students' learning, albeit earlier and more frequently.

Barry Lane, an educator, author, and humorist I met while working in New Delhi, India, in 2010, suggested during one of our many discussions that the term *formative assessment* be replaced with *informative assessment.* After all, the purpose of formative assessment is to inform learners about steps they need to take to improve their learning. (You may wish to view the video clip of our discussion at **go.solution-tree.com/instruction**.) Let's consider two case studies that illustrate how assessment for learning can inform students about what they have mastered and what they still need to improve in order to be successful on subsequent summative assessments.

"Bump It Up!"

In Kristeen's and Janice's grade 5 and 6 classes, students clearly understand the importance of feedback on formative work to enable them to "bump up" the quality of their writing. The Bump It Up Wall, inspired by colleagues from a Leading Student Achievement (LSA) workshop in London, Ontario, is a teaching tool that they use currently to improve writing forms and reading responses, and they hope to adapt it to mathematics. As they describe the process:

> To begin, we administer a diagnostic assessment to see what the students bring to the table. Then, as a teacher team, we look at their responses and select a cross-section of responses to view as a class. The focus here is to collaborate to identify what a level 3, or even 4, answer might look like. Through these discussions and feedback occurs some of the richest, most accountable talk.
>
> From there, we take the feedback and write level 1, 2, 3 and 4 sample responses with no more than three arrows indicating the next steps needed to bump up the responses. These are posted in an area where students can easily access the information. Students are encouraged to go to the wall, compare their responses to the samples provided, and bump up their work based on the next steps provided on the arrows. Students then submit their newly revised responses for teacher feedback.
>
> Generally, at this point, a new opportunity to practice the skill is provided. Students still have access to the wall as well as their diagnostic piece and the teacher feedback.
>
> Our goal of using this tool is to increase student achievement in various areas of writing and responding critically to texts. We hope that through multiple opportunities to practice this strategy, students will show a marked improvement in their tasks and will be more independent (gradual release of responsibility). Eventually, a summative assessment task is assigned for grading purposes.
>
> Throughout this process, we have noticed that our students have grown in confidence when accepting teacher feedback and moving through the revising/editing process. They are more willing to persevere to achieve their highest level of success, because they believe they can. They have experienced what it is like to reflect on their work and identify their next steps. (Kristeen Bunda and Janice Prangley, personal communication, January 10, 2011)

What better way is there to model excellence for students than the Bump It Up Wall? As Rick Stiggins noted many years ago (personal communication, May, 1990), "Most students can hit the target if they can see it clearly, and it stands still for them." But the most powerful feature of the Bump It Up Wall is that students are empowered to set and achieve their own improvement goals. This is assessment *as* learning at its best!

Mike's Mathematics Class

In his high school mathematics classes, Mike uses a combination of a rich performance task and a unit test to provide summative evidence of essential learning at the end of each unit. Because these two components comprise the major grading elements for each unit, Mike is eager for his students to be successful on both. But in his vocational mathematics courses, his students struggle to perform well on written tests. A few years ago, he instituted the practice of offering students the opportunity of completing an online ungraded practice quiz a week or so before a unit test. Students can complete the quiz at home on a computer in the middle of the night if they wish! Students receive immediate feedback from the assessment software as to which concepts and procedures they understood and got correct and which they got incorrect. Mike is able to log in to the program at any time to see how well an individual student, or the class as a whole, has performed. While the scores are not part of the students' grades, Mike and his students use the data from online quizzes to target those essential learnings that have not yet been mastered. Some of these data lead Mike to reteach some parts of the unit to the whole class, some data point to the need to focus on a specific concept or procedure that a group of students has not yet mastered, and some data point to the need for Mike to work with individual students on gaps in their learning.

When I asked Mike what percentage of his students chose to take advantage of the online ungraded quizzes, he replied, "By this point in the semester—late May—100 percent! But at the beginning of the semester, it may be between 40 percent and 60 percent. I don't force them. It's their choice. I let students discover for themselves that the ungraded quizzes help them do better on the unit tests."

As a follow-up question, I asked Mike if he had trouble getting students to do their best on tasks like the quizzes when they knew they would not be included in their summary grades.

"On the contrary!" Mike replied. "A lot of them ask, 'Why don't all teachers let us do practices first? That way, we can make mistakes and learn from them, instead of being punished for them.'"

This case study dispels the pervasive myth that middle and high school students will not engage in tasks if they don't count—that is, if they are not rewarded with grades. Crucial to Mike's success with this strategy is allowing his students to choose whether or not to take advantage of the pre-test quizzes. Over time, increasing numbers of students do participate in the ungraded practice quizzes, because they discover for themselves how instruction directed specifically at the mistakes they make in practice leads inevitably to improved performance in the "game." Such changes in practice often require a leap of faith. And while such endeavors will rarely meet with immediate success, involving a team of teachers, as Mike did, will enable you to collaborate in planning, implementing, observing, and modifying the components of a new strategy.

Quality Work

At a workshop for high school teachers, I asked my usual question to determine the needs of the group before beginning my session: "What are your major concerns concerning classroom assessment and grading?" The overwhelming response? "How do we get students to care enough to produce quality work?"

Granted, if we don't *demand* excellence from our students, many will be content to produce mediocre work. From my own experience, we can get high-quality work from all students if we constantly use these four questions to examine our own practice:

1. Do I ensure that *all* of the work I am asking students to do is worth their time and effort? In other words, is it meaningful, relevant, engaging, and authentic?

2. Do I *always* provide students with clear performance standards for their work? In other words, do they know what excellence looks like?

3. Do I *constantly* impress upon students that high-quality work takes time to produce? In other words, do I demand hard work from *all* students?

4. Do I *always* insist on excellence in the final product? In other words, do my students understand that anything less than each student's very best work is unacceptable?

You may be thinking, "There's nothing new here!" Maybe so, but in my experience, teachers who are able to reply affirmatively to all four questions, all of the time, are exceptional. (And I wasn't among them!)

Conclusion

Excellence is an overused and widely misunderstood goal in today's schools. Because teaching and learning is such a complex endeavor, it is ill-served by simplistic single measures such as test scores. Excellence in learning demands multiple measures, gathered over time, and involves numerous dimensions, including measures of understanding. These measures must be inclusive of all students, rather than focusing on the highest achievers. While current measures of success tend to focus on student outputs, teachers need to be cognizant of conditions that foster excellence in student learning. These include:

- A classroom climate that supports the learning of all students

- Effective and collaborative program planning

- An understanding by teachers and students of the different purposes served by assessment *for* learning and assessment *of* learning

- The expectation that all work submitted by students meet previously established standards

In classrooms where excellence thrives, teachers and students share a vision of success. This vision is reflected in the public display of rubrics, checklists, and student anchors. The latter may take the form of written work posted on walls, exemplary projects displayed on shelves, or videos of exemplary performance available for students to view. Student and teacher talk is characterized by phrases such as "Bump it up," "It's not quite there yet," "Quality is job number 1," and "I can do this." But most importantly, excellent classrooms are filled with optimism and belief, not excuses and blame.

CHAPTER 6

How Should I Assess Learning in the Mixed-Ability Class?

When teachers ask me how to assess learning in a class with a wide range of needs, I begin by referencing the work of Vygotsky (1978) and Wiliam and his colleagues (Leahy, Lyon, Thompson, & Wiliam, 2005). Combining the zone of proximal development model with assessment for learning principles, I suggest the following process:

1. Review the learning targets for the grade you are teaching. These will include content standards (knowledge and skills students are expected to learn) and may include performance standards (the level at which students are expected to demonstrate their learning). Your overall goal is to have all students demonstrating proficiency, independently, at grade level.

2. At the beginning of a term or semester, determine all students' current levels of understanding and skill proficiency with respect to these learning targets (preassessment).

3. Determine the gap between step 1 and step 2 for all students.

4. Based on the gaps between step 1 and step 2, establish appropriate learning targets for each student, and create manageable instructional groups.

5. Use a combination of instruction and formative assessment (descriptive, *not* evaluative) as you work with these groups to improve students' understanding and skills.

6. Continue to adjust the learning targets you set for groups and individuals in step 4 to ensure that all students are working within their zone of proximal development (ZPD).

7. Periodically, use benchmark or summative assessments that require students to demonstrate their levels of understanding and/or skills, as measured against the targets you set in step 4.

8. As a reporting period approaches, review anecdotal records, benchmarks, and summative data in order to communicate to students and parents about growth, progress, and/or achievement (see chapters 9 and 10, pages 123 and 141).

Yes, this is a lot of work! And it is challenging work. But the rewards are immeasurable in terms of both students' and teachers' sense of accomplishment. Key to the success of this process is that teacher and students understand that assessment's primary purpose is to *improve* learning and that they work together to achieve this goal. While measuring learning is ultimately necessary, this purpose is of secondary importance, especially to the struggling student. And assessment can only improve learning if it is descriptive, not evaluative—that is, if it is qualitative, not quantitative.

Understanding the Relationship Between Assessment for Learning and Assessment of Learning

If you were to ask me what I consider to be the most vexing problem I see in classroom assessment practice, it is the failure of many teachers to understand the difference between assessment designed to *improve* learning and assessment designed to *measure* it. I remember a dinner conversation in 1979 at the house of parents of a good friend with whom I attended teacher's college. The friend's father was a high school principal, and over dinner he asked, "So, Damian, after two weeks of your first term teaching, how many marks do you have for your students?" Learning, as I had, that the more data I had collected the better, I lied and replied, "Between four and six marks for each of my three classes." His smiling nod and words of approval suggested that I had passed the test!

Yes, I had learned that reliability is a function of the quantity of data gathered, so everything students did counted! But scoring everything students do or produce is bad practice for all students, and it can be particularly harmful to struggling students. Not surprisingly, when struggling students constantly receive low grades and scores, they see little reason to persevere.

Furthermore, scores signify to students and their parents that work is finished. Whether the work is of high, mediocre, or poor quality, once the teacher assigns a score to a piece of work, the message to the student is, "It's done."

Contrast this assessment practice with that employed by Liz. Liz is a high school science teacher who stamps every task she sets for her students as either "a practice" or "a game." Students know that their practice work will receive *only* comments—descriptive feedback from Liz that tells them what they have done well, where there are problems, and what they need to do to improve. Liz's students no longer expect to receive a numerical score on their practice work; rather, they understand that the purpose of practice work is improvement. On the other hand, their "games," which represent their best work, improve on the basis of feedback and receive either a series of scores for each of the assessment criteria or an overall score for the work as a whole.

Liz's classroom assessment routines are a consequence of the ground-breaking research by Paul Black and Dylan Wiliam (1998) that has repeatedly identified the power of formative assessment to improve learning for all students, but especially for students deemed to be at risk. Black and Wiliam write of the research they examined (1998, p. 3):

> Some of these studies exhibit another important feature. Many of them show that improved formative assessment helps the (so-called) low attainers more than the rest, and so reduces the spread of attainment whilst also raising it overall. One very recent study is entirely devoted to low attaining students and students with learning disabilities, and shows that frequent assessment feedback helps both groups enhance their learning (Fuchs et al., 1997).

Of course, many teachers—especially those working in the middle and high school grades—will say that students will not complete work if they're not going to receive grades. We saw the fallacy of this argument in Mike's mathematics class (chapter 5, page 70). Where does the fixation on the part of students and parents with grades and scores originate?

The association that students make between assessment and grades is not a naturally occurring phenomenon. It is a learned response, resulting from classroom practices that may begin as early as grade 2. I love to spend time in kindergarten or grade 1 classrooms, where a whole day can go by without my once hearing, "Does this count?" or "What's this assignment worth?" Instead, I see students and their teachers joyously involved in the thrill and discovery of learning as an end in itself! But all too soon, we teach children to associate learning with scores. A recent visit to a grade 3 class highlighted the problem for me. The class contained a rambunctious mix of twenty-six students. The teacher, Shelley, used a variety of strategies that included use of whole-class, paired, small-group, and individualized instruction. But what struck me was the constant demand from all students: "Miss, do I get a point for that?"

Whether students were writing in their exercise books, responding to oral questions, solving problems in mathematics, or tidying up their work spaces before recess, the question was the same: "Miss, do I get a point for that?"

And the reason for their demands was that Shelley did not move without her clipboard and class list. Throughout the day, she constantly entered points beside students' names as a reward for work completed, questions answered, and tasks completed.

At the end of the day, we met to debrief. I began with the positive elements that I had observed—Shelley's thorough preparation, her obvious care and commitment to all her students—but then I mentioned the points. Shelley quickly became defensive, saying, "You didn't like the points, did you?"

"Could we discuss this strategy, Shelley?" I asked.

"It works!" Shelley insisted.

"In what way?"

"My students are engaged."

Engagement is a cognitive or emotional response that derives from the motivation of completing work that students find intrinsically interesting, challenging, or meaningful and therefore worthy of their time and energy. Students willingly engage in thinking, decision making, and problem solving when they are invested in learning for its own sake. In Shelley's class, it appeared that her students' demands for points were externally motivated. Rather than being cognitively engaged, the students had become conditioned to work for points.

At the end of our chat, we agreed to disagree, but Shelley's final comment left me puzzled: "Oh well, they're very young. They'll grow out of this."

Unfortunately, the opposite is true: if children in grade 2 are already learning that the primary purpose for completing work is to be rewarded with points, it is no wonder that teachers in subsequent divisions tell me there is no chance students will complete formative tasks unless they are scored. While she clearly had the best interests of her students in mind, Shelley was unwittingly teaching them that school is not really about learning. It's about racking up maximum points with minimum effort! By awarding points for everything from tidying up the classroom before recess to demonstrating understanding of an important concept, Shelley is training these students to work for purely extrinsic rewards. It is no surprise that so many middle and high school teachers lament that their students will not complete any work unless it "counts."

But as we saw in the case of Mike's mathematics class, even high school students will happily complete work that does not receive a numerical score, provided that what they receive instead—helpful, descriptive feedback— helps them improve their learning. Consider the following reflections from grade 5 students who were asked to reflect on getting comments instead of grades at the end of the year.

Student 1—"I think that I have improved in my learning because in the starting of the year all I cared about was if I got on the honor roll and if I got As and Bs, but now I care about my learning.

"Next year, if I don't have a comment teacher like Ms. DeCosse, I will ask the teacher if he or she could give me a comment saying what I did well and what I can improve on."

Student 2—"This year I have liked marks, but comments have helped me know what I am good in writing and what I should work on for next time.

"That made me think more about my learning and not just about the marks. For next year, if a teacher does something and I don't get it, then I will ask, can you show me in another way?"

Student 3—"School had always come easily to me. I was proud of my continuing As and 4s. At the beginning I thought, Where's my mark? How do I know if I got an A? At the bottom of the page there was only a comment.

"It is close to the end of grade 5. Now I enjoy getting comments, not just marks. Comments give me something to improve on even if I got a 4. Comments also tell me some things that I'm good at or something I can be proud of.

"Getting comments makes me think harder and try to reach my learning goals. I can challenge myself, and it's not all about the mark. Now I'm thinking more about the meaning of my writing. I like getting comments, and I'm proud of my marks and my learning."

Source: Personal communication, Stacy DeCosse, J.A. Laird Elementary School, Invermere, British Columbia, September, 2008. Used with permission.

Much of my own work with teachers is devoted to helping them discover for themselves and their students how ongoing, descriptive assessment that relies upon words, not scores, has far greater potential to improve learning than does summative assessment. The following two case studies illustrate the kinds of excellent work, undertaken by teachers of their own volition, that I frequently encounter in my consulting.

Informative Self and Peer Assessment in Grade 3 Writing

During my visit to Claudette Oegema's grade 3 class, I observed her students deeply engaged in sophisticated self and peer assessment.

Claudette uses a combination of excellent teacher instruction and frequent opportunities for peer assessment to improve the writing skills of her grade 3 students. According to the following learning targets, which provide the focus for a series of lessons designed to improve expository writing skills, students should be able to:

1. Generate, gather, and organize ideas and information to write for an intended purpose and audience

2. Draft and revise their writing, using a variety of informational, literary, and graphic forms and stylistic elements appropriate for the purpose and audience

3. Use editing, proofreading, and publishing skills and strategies, and knowledge of language conventions, to correct errors, refine expression, and present their work effectively

The previous day, students had read a story that involved a game called bashball. They had then responded to the following writing prompt:

"What game does bashball remind you of? Use information from the narrative and your own ideas to support your opinion."

The goals of this particular lesson were:

• To improve students' self- and peer-assessment skills using written feedback

• To be able to improve written work on the basis of written feedback

The lesson began with Claudette and her students examining student work samples to review the elements they were to include in their written pieces and thus prepare them for the self- and peer-assessment task. Claudette's oral questioning, coupled with the A.P.E. Checklist (fig. 6.2, page 80), ensured that all students understood the assessment criteria.

Students worked in pairs, reading and assessing their own and each other's pieces. They used a combination of highlighters and anecdotal comments to identify each of the required elements, first on their own work and subsequently on the work of their peers. Figures 6.1 and 6.2 (page 80) feature a sample of the work produced, as well as a checklist.

What game does bashball remind you of? Use information from the narrative and your own ideas to support your opinion.

Bashball remind me of baseball because in bashball it has a ball and a wooden bat just like baseball.

In the text it say that bashball is like baseball because it has a ball and a wooden bat just like baseball.

_____

_____

_____

Bashball reminds me of baseball because in bashball it has a ball and a wooden bat just like baseball. In

the text it say "That in bashball your only have 3 trys like baseball. This remind me of bashball because my

sister and cozin and I've tried to set up a game of baseball.

_____

_____

_____

Figure 6.1: Student work based on the "bashball" story.

Moving around the classroom as they worked, I was impressed by the level of engagement demonstrated by *all* students, specifically:

- Students demonstrated commitment to self- and then to peer assessment as reflected in their time on-task.
- Students understood the tasks and knew what to do if they were uncertain about something.
- Students made frequent reference to the exemplar on the screen to clarify their own assessment work.
- Students were respectful of their peers as indicated by the way they interacted when discussing their written feedback to each other.

The teacher, Claudette, moved around the room, constantly monitoring students' work on the tasks and intervening when necessary.

A.P.E. Checklist—Self

Did I use three highlighters?	(Yes)	No
Do I have three sentences?	Yes	(No)
Did I start each sentence with a capital?	(Yes)	No
Did I use my pink words in my first sentence?	(Yes)	No
Did I prove my point? (Did I mention baseball?)	(Yes)	No
Did I make a self to text connection? (Did I talk about playing or watching baseball?)	Yes	(No)

I like how I *tryed my best* _____

_____

I need to work on *my text connections and my 3 sentences.*

_____

A.P.E. Checklist—Peer

Did your partner use three highlighters?	(Yes)	No
Do they have three sentences?	Yes	(No)
Did they start each sentence with a capital?	(Yes)	No
Did they use their pink words in the first sentence?	(Yes)	No
Did they prove their point? (Did they mention baseball?)	(Yes)	No
Did they make a self to text connection? (Did they talk about playing or watching baseball?)	(Yes)	No

I like how you *neat printing!* _____

_____

You need to work on *3 sentences.* _____

_____

_____

Figure 6.2: A.P.E. self and peer checklists.

While Claudette's approach focused on a single grade—grade 3—this next example illustrates how a kindergarden-to-grade-3 team sought to improve the teaching and assessment of writing across the primary division.

Support materials for Claudette Oegema's grade 3 language arts lesson can be found at **go.solution-tree.com/instruction** and in reproducible form in the appendix (page 169).

Assessment Begins in Kindergarten

There is no better way for teachers to improve their craft than to engage in action research. Recently, I had the opportunity to serve as consultant to a team of Canadian primary teachers who received provincial funding to investigate the teaching and assessment of writing in the primary grades. The impetus for the project came from three teachers' observations about the huge range of writing skills demonstrated by the children they taught. They chose to investigate this problem and set out to develop tools and strategies to address it. Following are some excerpts from their final report (Ault, Dawson, & MacCulloch, 2009, pp. 8–21):

> Our plan of action, therefore, was to develop our own writing continuum that would describe what primary children could reasonably be expected to achieve in writing at the end of each term for each grade (K–3). This would be augmented with student exemplars to clarify criteria for meaningful student feedback and to assist teachers with assigning grades at the end of each term. (p. 6)

The team identified the steps in its process as follows:

- Look at the curriculum and identify the modes of writing required for each grade.

- Identify criteria for assessing student writing with a focus on quality.

- Collect samples of student writing for each grade from other schools.

- Sort and map the samples to existing developmental tools (for example, First Steps) to see what is typical for each term and grade.

- Create a continuum based on this data. (p. 8)

The continuum evolved as the team's learning progressed. Figure 6.3 (page 82) is a portion of the continuum in its final form. Visit **go.solution-tree .com/instruction** to download the full continuum.

Achieve-ment Chart Criteria	Typical Skill Acquisition for Students in Kindergarten			Typical Skill Acquisition for Students in Grade 1		
	*SK— first term	SK— second term	SK— third term	Grade 1— first term	Grade 1— second term	Grade 1— third term
KNOWLEDGE & UNDER-STANDING	➡			➡		
Organization						
Structure, logi-cal order, and sequencing Effective beginning, satisfying end	Picture matches words.	Picture matches sentences.	Picture matches sentences.	Picture matches writing. Text tends to be in ran-dom order.	Picture shows some events. Has list-like sequence of events or details. • Evidence of a begin-ning • Some basic transitions (*next, then*) used correctly. Sentence parts linked (*and, so*).	Picture reflects essence of text. Most sen-tences in sequential order. • Beginning reflects main idea; evidence of an ending. • Most basic transitions (*next, then*) used correctly. • Most parts fit and make sense. Sentence parts linked (*and, so, because*). Title states topic.

*SK = Senior Kindergarten

Figure 6.3: Portion of the primary grade writing continuum.

Once the continuum was in its final form, the primary team was able to make the following claims:

> The Primary Grade Writing Continuum is a clear, concise, teacher-friendly instrument that:
>
> • Aligns provincial achievement criteria with the provincial writing curriculum and elements of writing in a framework of developmentally appropriate practice

- Describes the writing skills that most students should be able to demonstrate by the end of first, second, and third terms in grades kindergarten to 3, respectively, for a Level 3 or "B" *(Level 3 or B represents "proficiency" on the four-level provincial performance standard)*

- Provides criteria to facilitate effective assessment *for* learning (that is, student goals, checklists and rubrics, next steps and feedback) and assessment *of* learning (that is, summative, report card evaluation), with the goal of improving student success in literacy. (p. 14)

Here is an excerpt describing how the continuum (fig. 6.4, page 84) may be used to improve student writing in the primary grades:

> Ideally, the continuum works best when embedded in backward design and assessment for learning, where children have lots of opportunities to practice writing, receive effective feedback from teachers and peers, and time to implement that feedback. As an assessment for learning tool, the continuum can be used for diagnostic and formative assessment purposes. It also identifies the criteria that may be used for summative assessment of students' writing.
>
> In its diagnostic capacity, the continuum allows the teacher to establish a starting point for each student. After acquiring samples of student writing, the teacher starts at the current term, and moves forward or backward to determine where the student's skill level lies. For example, if a grade 2 student in the first term can write only four sentences, with a few incomplete, and tends to write in a list-like way, it is likely his or her skill level is around second-term, grade 1. The criteria for third term will provide next steps and direction for improvement (fig. 6.4, page 84).
>
> To facilitate formative assessment, teachers can use the continuum to communicate to students the goals they will be working toward. For example, using backward design planning, the teacher might say to his or her students the following, based on second term, grade 1: "We are going to learn how to organize our writing so that our ideas are in order and make sense. Our writing will have a beginning, a middle, and an end and some order words like first and next. At the end of our unit, we will use what we have learned to write an account of what we did on a snowy day." (p. 16)

Achievement Chart Criteria	Typical Skill Acquisition for Students in Grade 1		
	Grade 1— first term	Grade 1— second term	Grade 1— third term
KNOWLEDGE & UNDERSTANDING		→	
Organization Structure, logical order, and sequencing Effective beginning, satisfying end	Picture matches writing. Text tends to be in random order.	Picture shows some events. Shows list-like sequence of events or details. • Evidence of a beginning • Some basic transitions (*next, then*) used correctly. Sentence parts linked (*and, so*).	Picture reflects essence of text. Most sentences in sequential order and connected. • Beginning reflects main idea; evidence of an ending. • Most basic transitions (*next, then*) used correctly. • Most parts fit and make sense. Sentence parts linked (*and, so, because*). Title states topic.
	Detailed picture • Some simple labels Three complete sentences related to topic; may include some incomplete sentences. Main idea is recognizable and matches picture. • Limited detail (e.g. name, color, size)	Detailed picture • Simple labels Four complete sentences related to topic; may include a few incomplete sentences. Main idea is clear and matches picture. • Some details are important. Beginning evidence of simple critical thinking/creativity (e.g. imaginative idea)	Detailed pictures • Descriptive labels (*black dog*) Five or more sentences related to topic; an occasional incomplete sentence. Main idea is well defined and matches picture. • Most details are important. Some evidence of simple critical thinking/ creativity in writing (e.g. gives reasons)

Figure 6.4: Using the continuum for diagnostic assessment in organization and ideas.

The power of the writing continuum lies in its dual function as both an assessment and an instructional tool for teachers. The developmental design of the continuum allows for preassessment of students' writing skills that is descriptive, not evaluative. The specificity of the continuum provides clear and concise indicators for teachers and students to aim for, within grades and from grade to grade.

Scaffolding and Assessment

When assessment is formative, the teacher provides whatever support may be necessary to enable students to improve their learning. Whether this means providing additional probes when a student appears not to understand a question, providing a scaffolded version of a problem-solving task that reminds a student of the steps in the process, or some other support that enables the student to have some success on a given task, as long as the task is formative in nature, these strategies are appropriate. The teacher provides more or less scaffolding depending on the level of independence demonstrated by the student. Remember, these assessments are designed to improve learning, not to measure it.

However, when the assessment is summative, coming at the end of a prescribed instructional period, unit, or term, then the student must demonstrate his or her learning independently, and with all the demands of the task in place. If the child is unable to perform the task successfully, then further teaching and formative assessment will be necessary—what Paul Black and his colleagues describe as "the formative use of summative tests" (Black, Harrison, Lee, Marshall, & Wiliam, 2004, p. 53). Ideally, we want to determine how well a student is able to demonstrate learning without support. But notice the word *ideally*. Although assessments *of* learning are summative, we do not want to set up students for frustration and failure, so it would be inappropriate to suggest that scaffolding must never be provided for these tasks. However, given that our goal must be to have all students demonstrate essential learning at a specified level of performance, and to do so independently, we must plan to provide minimal or no scaffolding on summative tasks.

This guideline does not preclude the provision of learning aids to students who have been formally identified as having special needs. For example, a Braille text for the visually impaired learner is an aid to learning that we would always expect to provide. Scaffolding, on the other hand, refers to the strategies, accommodated materials, or oral prompts that are necessary to facilitate learning. The use of scaffolding should be temporary.

The Negative Impact of Scores and Grades

The preceding discussion has identified the importance of assessment that improves learning. Yet the psychometric tradition in assessment and evaluation has left educators with deeply held beliefs and habits with respect to the primacy of scores, letter or numerical grades, and percentage grades. Some of these habits have a devastating impact on students.

Recently, I was visiting a vocational high school. It was a warm spring Friday afternoon as I visited the last class of the day. This grade 10 history class was populated by a challenging mix of troubled adolescents. Midway through the class, the young male teacher showed a short video documentary depicting the historical events that the class had been studying. He provided students with a viewing and responding task to focus their attention during the video. This also provided him and me with a few minutes to discuss the achievements and challenges faced by various students in the class. Because students were to receive their interim achievement reports on this day, the teacher shared a number of these with me. (Arrangements for my research work in this school permitted access to student achievement data.)

Distressingly, many students had failing grades as a result of zeroes that had been assigned for work not submitted.

As the video came to an end, the teacher engaged the students in an excellent discussion about what they had seen and the responses they had made on their viewing and responding guides. The next phase of the lesson involved students taking turns going up to an interactive whiteboard to arrange events depicted in the video on a timeline. The lesson was engaging and well paced, and both the teacher and educational assistant interacted positively with the students. But then, with five minutes remaining until the bell to send students off into the Friday sunshine, the teacher called students by name and handed them their achievement reports. All students, including those who had received grades as low as 30 percent, left the classroom that day with no words of encouragement and no words of explanation to soften the blow.

Here was a young teacher who had excellent instructional and interpersonal skills, who understood the power of technology to reach adolescent learners, and who clearly was intent on teaching effectively. Yet a traditional, unsound, and insensitive grading and reporting process, coupled perhaps with his own lack of experience, resulted in his last action of the day potentially undermining much of what he had accomplished throughout the first term with these highly challenged adolescents.

What is the solution, and with whom does responsibility rest for changing this scenario?

First of all, administrators at both the district and school level must ensure that assessment and grading policies that are supportive of learning are in place and are followed by all teachers. I realize this is easier said than done, but fair practices by teachers originate with pedagogically sound policy. Such policies clearly indicate how teachers should respond when students do not complete essential assessment tasks. Simply put, when determining interim grades, if one or more critical tasks is missing from the body of evidence, then "incomplete" should appear on the report card in place of a summary grade. The incomplete notice is the stimulus for creating a completion plan—developed by the student, teacher, possibly the resource teacher, and possibly the parent—with the intent being to have the student complete all critical tasks prior to the next reporting period.

Let's explore the rationale behind this approach. When teachers develop high-quality assessment plans that comprise well-designed assessment tasks matched to essential learning, local and school policies must communicate to students the necessity of submitting *all* of the evidence necessary to certify their proficiency. I urge teachers to tell their students, "You won't receive your driver's license if, on the day of your in-car test, you tell the examiner to test you on everything except reversing because you could never master that competency!" As Douglas Reeves so eloquently states, "The appropriate consequence for failing to complete the assignment is to require the student to complete the assignment" (Reeves, 2004, p. 324).

Districts and schools in which I have been working lately are coming to this realization. For example, one district has instituted a "Just do it!" program in its high schools, immediately following interim report cards. Students are assigned before and after school and at lunch time to supervised work rooms, where school administrators provide support, assistance, and an appropriate degree of pressure to see that missing assessment tasks are completed. The messages to students must be clear: excellence is an expectation, not an option. Because every assessment task addresses certain of the essential learning targets in each course, every task must be completed before certification can occur.

While many current state and provincial policies send entirely different messages to students, I continue to be impressed by local initiatives that do *not* settle for mediocrity.

Conclusion

Most children enter kindergarten or first grade ready and eager to learn. Unfortunately, all too soon, young children learn that school is *not* primarily about learning; it's about accumulating maximum points. During the last decade, educators have discovered the power of assessment to improve learning, not simply to measure it. Unfortunately, decades of the psychometric tradition have created a mythology of measurement that has convinced students, parents, and teachers that anything that can be taught and learned can be measured. One sad consequence of this myth has been a generation of learners who engage in schoolwork primarily to gain extrinsic rewards or to avoid punishment.

Educators have a responsibility to challenge the mythology of measurement by reframing assessment's primary purpose: that is, to improve learning. To accomplish this, teachers, students, and parents need to understand that there are different kinds of assessment, having different purposes and requiring different responses from students and teachers. We identify the purpose of assessment *for* learning as focusing and improving learning, whereas assessment *of* learning determines how much learning has occurred by the end of a prescribed instructional period. Assessment *for* learning must include descriptive feedback to the learner. Furthermore, assessment *for* learning is more effective when it does *not* include grades and scores.

The mythology of measurement has also perpetuated the misconception that only the teacher has the knowledge and skills to assess student learning. The most serious consequence of this mistaken belief has been to disempower students. Again, the natural propensity of young children to assess the quality of their own work and that of their peers is snuffed out as they become ever more dependent on teachers to mark their work. This trend has to be reversed. "What did I get?" or "How did I do?" must give way to statements like "I met the first three criteria on the rubric, but I still think I need to work on my organization." Self- and peer assessment are essential processes by which students come to internalize performance standards, and thereby to know precisely what they must do to improve their learning and the quality of their work.

When teachers discover the power of assessment to improve learning, they begin to see the potential of low and failing scores to undermine learning. Assessment that occurs during the learning process must inform students about what they are doing well, what they need to improve, and what they need to do differently to achieve their goals. A low or failing score received during learning is more likely to discourage than to motivate the learner. Replacing such scores with informative feedback is simply good teaching.

CHAPTER 7

How Should Assessment and Instruction Connect in the Mixed-Ability Class?

No matter which state, province, or country I go to work in these days, differentiated instruction is on everyone's priority list. But while district and school administrators agree on the importance of DI, many teachers I meet voice either skepticism or even cynicism at what they view as the latest educational panacea. For this reason, I'm increasingly using Tomlinson and McTighe's term *responsive teaching* (2006) as an alternative to *differentiated instruction.* Responsive teachers understand that effective teaching must begin with assessing the prior knowledge and skill levels of their students, they accept that these assessments will reveal a variety of learning needs, and they understand that while their long-range plans will identify broad learning targets common to all students, they will need to tailor and constantly adapt day-to-day instruction to help all students realize their potential.

If teachers are to respond to the differing needs of their students, they must first get to know them as individuals. This cannot happen in classrooms that are teacher-centered and teacher-driven. If there is a common denominator to classes I visit in which large numbers of students are disengaged, it is that learning is determined, directed, and controlled by the teacher. And in academic classes—as distinct from the performing arts, technologies, and other such offerings—this means that:

- Desks are arranged in rows all of the time.
- The teacher is doing most of the talking.
- The textbook is the program of study.

- Students have little or no say in what they are learning.

- Talk and movement are discouraged.

Beginning With Students' Strengths and Deficits

Highly effective teachers simply "get kids." They look at children and adolescents not as ill-formed adults, but as young human beings who differ in significant ways from mature adults. Andrew is just such a teacher. He plans his program, develops units, and prepares lesson plans with his students in mind. The students (all teenage boys) in Andrew's "transitions" class—a special program to help students who have been unsuccessful in the middle grades to make a successful transition into high school workplace courses—exhibit the following characteristics:

- They lack confidence about their ability to learn.

- They have a history of failure or very poor achievement.

- They like to talk.

- They like to move around.

- They respond well to competition.

- They enjoy humor.

- They have short attention spans.

- They have poor organizational skills.

- Some have poor role models at home.

Andrew understands, intuitively, that if he is to be successful in his task as teacher and his students successful in theirs as learners, he must plan with this set of characteristics in mind. I have spent a significant amount of time with Andrew, both in his classes and chatting with him outside of class. Not once have I heard him express disappointment in his students or speak of them in other than positive terms. He believes in their capacity to be successful, just as they believe in his ability to teach them. It is precisely because he plans with his students in mind that he is rarely disappointed by them. For example, he knows they love to move around, so he doesn't plan lessons that require students to sit for a long time. Instead, he posts an agenda for each day's lesson and identifies the point at which students will take turns coming to the interactive whiteboard. He knows they love to talk, so he provides numerous opportunities throughout each lesson for students to talk among themselves in order to deepen learning. Andrew's students love to compete, so he routinely uses competitive games to consolidate or review learning. He knows that humor can break the ice, lighten the mood, provide comic relief after a discipline problem, and generally enrich the student-teacher relationship. He places minimal expectations on his students regarding homework because many of their home lives are unstable. Similarly, because most of his students need support with organizing time and materials, he provides and constantly adjusts scaffolding for each student, with the goal being independence demonstrated by all.

Empowering Students

If students are to learn deeply and sustainably, they must be empowered. By that I mean the teacher must hold them accountable for learning by transferring much of the responsibility for teaching, thinking, and problem solving to them. As the title of a recent book by Robyn Jackson reminds teachers, *Never Work Harder Than Your Students* (Jackson, 2009). And yet, in so many of the classrooms I visit, teachers are doing just that. They are doing most of the talking, most of the thinking, most of the questioning, most of the assessment, most of the correcting of errors, most of the problem solving, and hence, most of the learning! Is it any wonder that so many teachers feel overwhelmed and so many students are disengaged? For all teachers of all grades, no understanding is more enduring than the principle of "gradual release of responsibility" (Pearson & Gallagher, 1983). In other words, a teacher's greatest responsibility is to make herself unnecessary to learning.

One high school visit provided a compelling contrast of student empowerment. The first class I visited was grade 11 science. After viewing a short film about the solar system, the teacher initiated a question-and-answer session, presumably to assess students' understanding. She asked all of the questions, and only a very small number of students contributed answers. As I often do, I used my stopwatch to record student and teacher "air time." In this twenty-minute session, the teacher spent most of the time talking. Of the twenty-eight students, nine participated in the question-and-answer session, and each of them had between ten and thirty seconds of air time. These nine students certainly had to think both before and during the time they were talking, and they were probably learning something. But what of the other nineteen students? How much were they learning as they sat silently in the classroom? How many of them were attending to what was being said? Admittedly, I didn't have any evidence to answer this question. Some students who did not actively participate may have been listening to and learning from the teacher and their peers, but it is also likely that many were disengaged.

It might be argued that the teacher will have evidence of who was attending when she has the class write a test or complete some other assessment task related to the film and follow-up discussion. However, for many students, the test may indicate, too late, that they were not attending and therefore not learning. Classroom routines need to change to demand that all students are attending and are engaged at all times. This is why Dylan Wiliam and his colleagues describe the most effective assessment as that which occurs "minute by minute and day by day" (Leahy et al., 2005, p. 18).

Which takes us into the second classroom I visited that day. I first noticed that all of the student desks were arranged in pods of four. Because I had entered the class partway through the lesson, Julie, the teacher, explained to me the focus for learning—she was able to do this because students were busily engaged in collaborative problem solving. This class was an applied (vocational) grade 10 class. Some of these students would go to college or for professional training, and others, who were not academically inclined, would go directly into the workplace. The mathematics curriculum they were working on was practical and applied. The lesson for this day dealt with problem solving related to surface area and volume. Here is an outline of the lesson:

1. Students work on a group problem-solving task using manipulatives.

2. Teacher leads the whole class in discussion about what they know and what they are struggling with.

3. Students work on the "aquarium" task (fig. 7.1) individually but are encouraged to consult their group members whenever necessary. The problem may be solved using either the formula for surface area or the formula for volume. Each method yields a different answer.

4. Measurement assessment—Students collaborate with group members to complete the task.

5. Students reflect on their knowledge by applying it to a new situation: "When painting a room, both volume and surface area measurements are involved. Explain how."

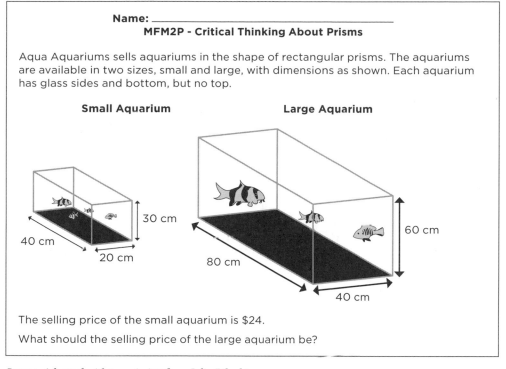

Name: _____

MFM2P - Critical Thinking About Prisms

Aqua Aquariums sells aquariums in the shape of rectangular prisms. The aquariums are available in two sizes, small and large, with dimensions as shown. Each aquarium has glass sides and bottom, but no top.

Small Aquarium   **Large Aquarium**

30 cm

40 cm

20 cm

60 cm

80 cm

40 cm

The selling price of the small aquarium is $24.

What should the selling price of the large aquarium be?

Source: *Adapted with permission from Julia Bilenkis.*

Figure 7.1: Aquarium task.

The most striking feature of this class was how much time *all* students spent talking about mathematics. At each stage of the lesson, students talked to each other in their four-person pods to raise questions, clarify understanding, consolidate their learning, brainstorm approaches to problems, validate each other's learning, and assess each other's strategies and solutions. Materials to support this lesson may be downloaded at **go.solution-tree.com /instruction** and found in reproducible form in the appendix (page 170).

I sat in with several groups to assess the depth of their understanding. Following is a transcription of the dialogue I had with one group as they solved the aquarium problem.

> **Author**: Could one of you explain to me what you have to do here?
>
> **First Student**: We have to apply what we've learned about solving problems about surface area and volume to figure out how much to charge for the big aquarium.
>
> **Author**: As I look at your work, I can see different answers. Surely only one of them can be right?

Second Student: No, you get a different answer if you use the formula for surface area to solve the problem than if you use the formula for volume.

Author: Okay, but is one answer better than the other?

Third Student: It depends on whether you're the store owner or the customer. If you're the store owner, then you'd want to calculate a higher cost for the large aquarium. But if you're the customer, you'd want the lower price.

Author: Of course! You folks really understand this stuff, don't you?

As I moved from group to group, regardless of which students I questioned, all were able to explain their strategies and their thinking. I was amazed!

In chatting with Julie, she explained that all of the mathematics classes in this school utilized the four-students per group seating plan and that students were empowered to be resources for each other in all classes.

Later that day, while visiting a grade 11 university level course, I saw for myself how this student-centered approach was employed with a more theoretical curriculum.

Grade 11 Mathematics Lesson on Functions

The focus of this lesson was to introduce the concept of functions. The teacher began the class by having students do a gallery walk to examine and assess the mind maps that each group had created to summarize its learning from the previous unit. Students were instructed to provide written feedback to at least three of the groups. Their feedback had to identify at least one strength, one weakness, and a suggestion for improvement.

C. J. then introduced today's lesson by asking, "What is the title of our textbook?" Students responded as one, saying, "*Functions.*" C. J. continued by introducing the day's lesson goal: "By the end of today's class, you will all understand what a function is." The lesson commenced with the teacher projecting on the screen several sets of relationships. She asked the students, "Which of these are functions, which are not, and how do you know?"

No hands went up! Instead, without prompting, all students began immediately to discuss the examples in their groups. Discussion was lively, animated, and not without disagreement! The teacher then asked for spokespeople from each group to share their conclusions with the class. Consensus emerged quickly. The teacher then projected a new set of relationships onto the screen, specifically intended to undermine the conclusions that she clearly knew the class would reach, based on the first set of examples. Throwing this wrench in the works increased students' engagement significantly. Over the course of the next twenty minutes, by presenting the class with increasingly challenging sets of examples, C.J. succeeded in having the groups deduce their own understanding of the characteristics of functions—and they had great fun doing it! The teacher moved her students from a simplistic, faulty understanding of functions to a deeper, sophisticated understanding. From my point of view as observer, the students had much more air time than C.J., and all were equally involved in talking, thinking, and thereby learning. In short, they were working much harder than their teacher.

I asked C.J. how she had brought her students to the point at which they view their peers as no lesser sources of information than their teacher. "This is how I've always taught," she told me. "At the beginning of the semester, I explain how the class is going to operate. Sure, it takes time to get them used to my style—less me and more them, solving problems collaboratively, self- and peer assessing, and so on. But as you can see, they're comfortable now." C.J. is aided in her approach by a department head and colleagues who share her commitment to empowering students. In every mathematics class that I visited at this school, from grade 9 to grade 12, desks were arranged in pods of four, and students spent as much, if not more time, speaking to each other as teachers spent talking to the class.

This raises the question of how students should be grouped.

Grouping Strategically

I am frequently asked how to group students for instructional and assessment purposes: "Is it better to group students homogeneously or heterogeneously, according to ability?" My response is always, "It depends on your purpose." No single type of grouping is best. Teachers must group students strategically, according to the kind of learning that needs to occur. For example, in the grade 10 mathematics class described earlier, if Julie has just introduced a new procedure and assigns a small number of practice questions to consolidate learning, she pairs students who have demonstrated strong math skills in previous units with students who are struggling. Later in the same lesson, when Julie has gathered evidence of students' differing levels of mastery of the new procedure, she forms homogeneous groups of four, so that those who have mastered the procedure can work more creatively, perhaps challenging each other with their own questions. Meanwhile, she works with small groups of challenged students, adjusting the work she asks them to do, as well as the amount of support she provides, in order to guide them toward mastery of the procedure.

Notice that in each case, Julie relies upon assessment data to form the groups. Early in the lesson, she relies upon preassessment data to create mixed-ability pairings; later in the lesson, she uses formative data from their current work to form homogeneous groups that will enable all students to work within their zone of proximal development.

In each instance, Julie is establishing who works with whom. If we accept that students can and should be learning resources for each other, then it follows that only the teacher has access to the necessary assessment data to group students effectively—that is, in ways that maximize learning for all. Granted, we may permit responsible, senior high school students to self-select groups, provided that we observe such groups to be functional. This is yet one more instance where teachers must use data about their students, combined with professional judgment, to make wise decisions that optimize learning for all students.

When I asked high school teacher Michelle how she manages grouping in her science classes, she replied:

> I group students intentionally, according to my purpose, but always to ensure a safe, secure, and supportive environment for learning. Sometimes I group them homogeneously, sometimes, heterogeneously; sometimes by interest, sometimes by learning style, sometimes by readiness. By me grouping them, they're better able to support each others' learning than when I used to let them choose their own groups. (M. McCutcheon, personal communication, March 8, 2010)

The Differentiated Lesson: Begin With a Common Plan

Concerns about prep time and manageability are two oft-cited reasons I hear for teachers *not* differentiating instruction. Middle-grades teacher Kim Savoie has mastered lesson planning in the mixed-ability classroom. Kim teaches mathematics, science, and language arts to a combined grade 7/8 class. As if having two grades in the same class were not challenge enough, Kim also has a wide range of ability within these two grade levels. But throughout the time I spent with her, she remained calm and confident in her ability to ensure that all of her students were learning to think, understand major concepts, and develop essential skills. What does Kim know that so many of her colleagues appear not to know? She begins with a common approach to long-range planning, unit planning, and lesson design. This is because she understands that *all* of her students must acquire and demonstrate the same essential learning: enduring understandings and essential skills. But she also understands and accepts that different groups of students will need to take different routes to reach this common destination—yes, it's the bicycle tour! Understanding these two principles guides Kim in her planning. For example, as she plans a lesson, she is clear about which elements of the lesson will be common to all students and which elements will need to be differentiated, according to students' needs, learning preferences, and interests. This is illustrated in the following model lesson.

1. Identify learning goal (common to all)
2. Activate prior knowledge and experience; hook and engage (common to all)
3. Diagnostically assess prior knowledge (common to all)
4. Present new learning (common to all or differentiated)
5. Check for understanding orally (common to all or differentiated)
6. Practice new learning and scaffold new learning (differentiated)
7. Self- and/or peer assess practice work (differentiated)
8. Review and consolidate learning; tie back to learning goal (common to all or differentiated)
9. Apply new learning to new context (differentiated)
10. Assess learning (differentiated)(Cooper, 2006, p. 213)

These lesson elements may be common to all or differentiated, depending on the point in the unit where the lesson occurs or on the results of the diagnostic assessment. For example, if the lesson is near the beginning of a unit, the diagnostic assessment in step 3 may indicate that students should be grouped on the basis of need and that quite different new learning should be presented to each of these groups. On the other hand, if the differences among the groups of students involve the depth of understanding or level of skill proficiency with respect to similar material, steps 4, 5, and 8 are more likely to be common to all.

Scaffolding: Why? Who? What? When? How?

Scaffolding serves an essential purpose on a work site: it supports workers and materials while a building is under construction. But scaffolding is temporary and unattractive; it is never intended to be permanent. These features are important as we apply the scaffolding metaphor to learning.

Scaffolding in the classroom—strategies and materials to support students' learning and progressively lead them to independence—takes many forms. These include:

- Simplified texts that present the same material but at a lower reading level
- More explicit instructions to cue students to follow steps in a procedure
- A less demanding task in terms of scope, breadth, depth, or complexity
- Additional prompts, either oral or written, to elicit student response

While providing scaffolding to support learning is a feature of any effective learning environment, teachers must always remain aware of the temporary nature of such supports. We should expect to provide plenty of scaffolding to some students early in the instructional process; however, evidence of deep learning depends on students' abilities to demonstrate understanding and skills autonomously—without scaffolding.

In classrooms where several students exhibit special needs or one or two students exhibit particular exceptionalities, an educational assistant (EA) often provides critical support to students and the teacher. In my own teaching career, I have had the pleasure of working with many EAs who contributed immeasurably to learning in my classes. If educational assistants have a fault, however, it is that they care too much for students. This overabundance of care can manifest itself in the EA's providing too much help, doing the thinking for the student, or creating the impression that students have mastered a skill or concept when they haven't. Teachers must, therefore, ensure that EAs see their primary role being to foster student independence.

What Does Effective Scaffolding Look Like?

In *The Differentiated Classroom* (1999), her groundbreaking work on differentiated instruction, Tomlinson presents what she calls "the equalizer," a simple yet highly effective tool for helping teachers adjust the level of complexity of instructional tasks to suit students' differing needs. The equalizer is a useful metaphor that refers to a device used with audio systems to achieve a satisfactory sound by compensating for distortions in each channel. In the classroom, the equalizer allows variables to be adjusted so that each student faces an equal level of challenge with respect to a given task. The equalizer also represents each variable as a continuum, enabling teachers to adjust levels to suit students' needs. The following set of five variables identifies elements of instruction and assessment that may need to be equalized:

1. Students' ability to transfer new knowledge and skills

2. Students' representation of what they have learned

3. Students' ability to apply new learning creatively

4. The level of direction required by students

5. The complexity of problems to be solved and tasks to be completed

The equalizer helps teachers decide how much scaffolding to provide for students to ensure that they are challenged yet supported. In figure 7.2 (page 100), the far left side of the continuum represents the most scaffolding, whereas the far right side represents the least.

Naturally, teachers can expect that struggling learners will require more scaffolding to be in place longer than will students who master concepts and skills easily. Nevertheless, the use of scaffolding must *not* alter or undermine the overall learning target or standard to be taught. To extend the metaphor, use of the audio equalizer does not change the station or the particular piece of music being played; it simply compensates for imbalances among frequency ranges. In the classroom, Tomlinson's equalizer is a useful tool to guide a teacher's adjustment of one or more instructional elements so that *all* students are able to play the intended piece of music (demonstrate achievement of desired outcomes). The equalizer should *not* result in struggling or highly able students playing different pieces (that is, pursuing different curriculum targets). However, there are two exceptions to this principle:

1. When a student, by virtue of an exceptionality, is unable to demonstrate learning outcomes, even at a lower grade level, and requires a unique program designed to meet his or her needs

2. When a gifted or highly able learner has demonstrated proficiency on the specified learning targets for a given program and is provided with an individualized set of learning outcomes designed to challenge the student appropriately

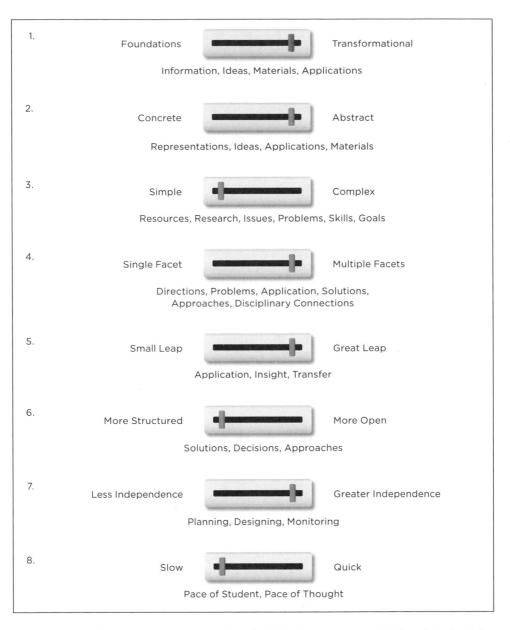

Source: How to Differentiate Instruction in Mixed-Ability Classrooms, 2nd ed. *(p. 47), by Carol Ann Tomlinson, Alexandria, VA: ASCD. © 2001 by ASCD. Reprinted with permission. Learn more about ASCD at www.ascd.org.*

Figure 7.2: The equalizer: a tool for planning differentiated lessons.

This emphasis on the need for thoughtful, careful use of a tool like the equalizer is based on my personal experience of visiting countless classrooms in which differentiated instruction is interpreted to mean merely providing students with plenty of choices: choices about what they will learn, how they will learn, and what products they will produce to demonstrate their learning. While flexibility and choice are fundamental elements of differentiated instruction, they are *not sufficient* to ensure learning. If teachers, working collaboratively with their students, are to make effective instructional choices that further learning, they must first have sufficient data relating to each of the dimensions on the equalizer. Such data enable the teacher to accommodate or modify a student's program, while preserving the integrity of the learning targets.

In this regard, Linda Gregg has some simple, yet sage advice for teachers working with students who struggle to perform at grade level:

> We can choose a variety of materials and methods to teach each skill defined in the standard, but proficiency in those specific skills and abilities remains a common landmark along the road to proficiency. For example, Julia, the seventh-grade student who reads at the third-grade level, can still learn to paraphrase, analyze, evaluate, and make predictions—but she will be more successful in acquiring those skills if her teacher uses third-grade materials that she can read and comprehend. To provide the necessary content knowledge, the teacher can then present seventh-grade materials in other formats: computer programs, audio tapes, videos, or assistive technology readers. Julia would then be able to apply skills to this material that she first learned using material at her lower reading ability level. This strategy is a dynamic way to quickly help students with special needs move forward and fill in the gaps in their learning, but requires skillful assessment of the student's content knowledge, learning style, background knowledge, and skills prior to direct instruction. (Gregg, 2007, p. 170)

Gregg's advice is critical for all teachers: many students struggle because they are frustrated both by their skill deficits *and* by unfamiliar subject content. Responsive teachers focus first on improving skills by simplifying content, either using resources from a lower grade level or selecting resources tailored to the student's interests. As the skills improve, the responsive teacher gradually increases the complexity of the content. Unfortunately, many teachers feel constrained by grade-specific content, believing that it is their duty to have all students master the same material. But if students lack basic literacy skills—in particular reading skills—they will never master required content! I spend a great deal of my time giving teachers permission to be flexible and responsive to students' needs. At the end of the day, it doesn't matter how much content the teacher has covered if results indicate that students haven't learned the material. And all too often, the lack of learning can be explained by deficits in students' skills.

Conclusion

If instruction is to be effective for all learners in a mixed-ability class, it must be responsive. Responsive teachers begin by getting to know their students as individuals, and then operate on the premise that effective teaching will, of necessity, be flexible to meet differing needs. Responsive teaching begins with a commitment to establishing positive working relationships with students. When teachers take the time to relate personally to their students, they gain knowledge about each learner that, when combined with achievement data and other measures, enables them to tailor instruction to meet everyone's needs.

Responsive teachers also understand that student engagement in learning is maximized when students are empowered. Students become empowered and engaged when they perceive learning to be worthwhile. Today's students demand relevance. They live in a fast-paced, stimulating world and expect their classrooms to reflect this world. And while students need to understand that not all work in school can or, indeed, should be fun, they have a right to expect that all work they are required to do is worthy of their time and energy. Teachers can dramatically increase the relevance of assigned work when they ask two simple questions:

1. Does this work have a connection to the world beyond the classroom? If not, could I change the task so that it does (for example, by reworking the task as a simulation, a role-play, or by using current events)?

2. How can I frame this work so that students have input and thereby take ownership of the work?

Far too much of the work that goes on in schools is determined, owned, and controlled by teachers. Is it any surprise, therefore, when students respond with disinterest, disengagement, and a "who cares?" attitude? Outside of the school day, learners of all ages are taking increasing control over their own lives. We set ourselves up for frustration and failure if we expect children and adolescents to surrender their autonomy in school each day and let teachers make all the decisions for them.

This leads to the question of instructional design. Teacher talk remains the dominant instructional style in the majority of classrooms that I visit.

However, in classrooms where time on-task and assignment completion are maximized and tardiness, truancy, and behavioral problems are minimized, I observe students learning as much from each other as they do from their teacher. The teachers in these classes also understand the importance of strategic grouping. Learning is optimized and behavioral problems minimized when teachers group students purposefully, according to the task at hand. At times, this requires homogeneous grouping, but at other times, students need to be grouped heterogeneously.

Because responsive teaching demands flexibility, teachers need to approach differentiation with a clear sense of which parts of a unit or lesson will be common to all students and which will require differentiation. Effective approaches to differentiation include the following elements:

- Common essential learning targets for all students

- Flexible approaches to instruction and skillful selection of resources to address differing needs

- High-quality assessments that are matched to the common essential learning targets but adapted to suit the variability in students' skills and understanding

With these elements in place, responsive teachers also understand the role that scaffolding plays in supporting learning. They anticipate the need to constantly monitor and adjust the amount of scaffolding provided to an individual or group during the learning process. And they understand that because the overarching goal of their teaching is to have all students working at or above grade level while independently demonstrating proficient achievement, they must progressively reduce the amount of scaffolding. From an assessment perspective, this often means considerable scaffolding during formative assessment, with the aim of little or no scaffolding when summative assessment occurs.

CHAPTER 8

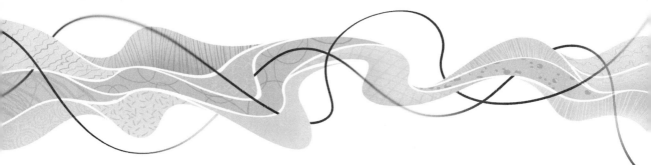

How Should Assessment Be Matched to Students' Needs?

Unfortunately, when it comes to assessing learning in the mixed-ability classroom, many teachers seem to believe that differentiation involves nothing more than offering students a smorgasbord of choices to demonstrate their learning. For example, in a senior English class, students had just finished reading the short story "The Machine Stops" by E. M. Forster and were presented with an array of options for demonstrating their learning. These included:

- Compare the original text with a comic-style adaptation.
- Present the climactic scene dramatically.
- Produce a piece of art to represent a key event.
- Answer a series of comprehension questions.

The teacher was confident that he had differentiated the assessment task with respect to Gardner's multiple intelligences (Gardner, 1983). But I had three questions to ask of the assessment options:

1. What essential learning do you intend to assess through this task, regardless of which option students chose?
2. What common assessment criteria will be applied to each of the choices to ensure consistency with respect to the evidence of learning demonstrated?
3. Are students always permitted to choose their preferred task—the one that aligns with their strongest learning modality?

A frequent response that I see to Gardner's concept of multiple intelligences and, more recently, to Carol Tomlinson's (2001) work on differentiation, is to simply let students choose the work they would like to produce from a menu of "fun" but often poorly designed options.

Metaphorically speaking, this approach is akin to parents who take their children to a restaurant that features an extensive buffet and then allow them to choose whatever they like and return to the buffet for the same food item as often as they want. Many children would choose only desserts! By contrast, responsible parents instruct their children to select a balanced set of food items, including all food groups. When a child protests that he or she hates broccoli, the parent quietly but firmly insists that the child must try at least a small portion of one of the green vegetables.

All too often, I encounter differentiated assessment tasks that entirely undermine the integrity of a given learning target. For example, consider the following curriculum outcome from a grade 11 history syllabus, the corresponding assessment task, and the differentiated version of the task:

- **Curriculum outcome**—"Discuss the human toll of the Depression, natural disasters, and unwise agricultural practices and their effects on the depopulation of rural regions and on political movements of the left and right, with particular attention to the Dust Bowl refugees and their social and economic impacts in California." (Klingensmith, 2000, p. 167)

- **Assessment task**—Students will review their learning from lessons, assigned readings, and their own research, and write a well-reasoned persuasive essay in which they discuss one or more of the cause-and-effect relationships identified in this learning outcome.

- **Differentiated task for struggling writers**—Students may prepare a collage or poster depicting one of the events identified in this learning outcome.

In no way does this differentiated task provide evidence of the stated learning target. The original task has the potential to assess students' reading, research, critical thinking, organizational, and communications skills. The differentiated task assesses students' ability to locate pictures and paste them on a piece of Bristol board! This is not an exaggerated example. It is typical of so-called differentiation practices in many schools. And yes, the collage is often the differentiated option of choice!

A colleague of mine recalled coming home one evening to find his daughter and a friend blowing up balloons. When he asked why, his daughter said, "We're working on our summative project for *Fifth Business*." When my colleague asked what the balloons had to do with their study of this novel, he was told, "We could choose a project on any of the themes in the book. We chose circuses."

He then asked, "Yes, but what learning are you supposed to show with this circus project?"

"Oh, anything really. So we thought we'd just turn the classroom into a circus ring. That's what the balloons are for."

These examples highlight the need for guidelines to help teachers as they differentiate the processes and the products that students will engage in and create as evidence of essential learning. These guidelines include:

1. Identify the essential learning to be demonstrated by *all* students.

2. Review the strengths, needs, interests, and learning profiles of your students.

3. Identify an appropriate menu of assessment processes or products matched to your students' profiles, ensuring that *all* of these will provide evidence of essential learning.

This is not to suggest that a menu of assessment processes and products cannot be developed before the term or semester begins. Experienced teachers continually add to these menus over time. But the specific menu that is offered to a given class will differ according to the profiles of the students in that class.

The teacher who is skilled in differentiation theory and practice similarly guides her students, over the course of a unit or term, into choosing different kinds of assessment tasks. Some of these will play into their strengths, while others will lead to improvement because they involve a greater challenge.

Planning Assessment Tasks With Your Students in Mind

Recall the case study from chapter 1 (page 13) in which Helen, a fifth-grade teacher, was introducing a research project to her students. The task had been designed to engage students in independent research about illnesses and diseases affecting the bodily systems of human beings. You may recall that as we chatted over lunch, Helen told me she was ready to quit because, in her words, "Probably two-thirds of my students either won't be able to do a good job on this project or else won't be bothered to—and it's always like this. I'm so frustrated!"

I suggested a common planning process to her that was responsive to the range of knowledge and skills demonstrated by her students. The approach I suggested to Helen is commonly called tiering (Strickland, 2007).

Tiering

Tiering involves designing an assessment task and then adapting it for different groups of students in order to present them with a version of the task that is matched to their current levels of skill and knowledge. From a manageability perspective, establishing three versions of the same task—not thirty!—is reasonable. The initial task should be designed to match at-grade expectations; the first adaptation would then be made for students who require a less demanding task; the second adaptation would be made for students who will be appropriately challenged by a more complex task. Pedagogically sound tiering *must* begin with clarity of learning targets for *all* students. Simply because some students may have more difficulty completing an assessment than others is *not* reason to change the learning targets for those students. Instead, the teacher must adjust the demands of the task to suit the strengths and needs of different groups of students.

A word of caution! Tiering is not to be confused with layering the curriculum. In the layered curriculum model, high school students select to work at one of three levels of curriculum complexity for a unit of study—level C, B, or A. Corresponding assessment tasks are provided at each level. Students choosing to work at a given level in effect enter into a contract to receive a grade of C, B, or A for the unit. There are several problems with this approach: first, the essential learning differs for each of the three levels. Students contracting to complete C work do not acquire the essential knowledge and skills associated with work at the A and B levels. Second, the model has the potential to reinforce norm-referenced attitudes about high and low achievers.

By contrast, the template shown in figure 8.1 is useful to ensure that the integrity of curriculum targets is maintained when tiering a corresponding assessment task. In this example, I have taken Helen's grade 5 science task and adapted it to suit the learning profiles of her students.

Notice how the degree of structure provided by the teacher varies significantly according to the three levels. The tiered task includes the research process that students will follow, as well as the products they will be required to generate as evidence of their learning.

Enduring Understandings: Understand how the different body systems are interconnected

Essential Skills: Research, organization, communication

Specific Knowledge and Skills: It is expected that students will

- Describe the basic structure and functions of the human respiratory, digestive, circulatory, skeletal, muscular, and nervous systems

- Explain how the different body systems are interconnected

- Generate and answer several questions to investigate how body systems are integrated, for example: How are the various systems connected to each other? Could one system live without the other systems? If not, why not?

- Demonstrate various ways in which body systems work together, using role plays, posters, and/or 3-D representations

Note: The assessment task is one of many that, taken together, will provide evidence of all of these outcomes.

© 2011 Province of British Columbia. All rights reserved. Reprinted with permission of the Province of British Columbia. www.ipp.gov.bc.ca

Overview of Task: Students will select a specific disease of the human body to research. They will present their findings using one of several presentation media. The research and presentation task has been tiered to suit different strengths and needs of students.

Assessment Criteria: A common rubric is provided for all versions of the task. Areas assessed include

- Research—posing questions, locating and using resources to answer questions, organizing materials to answer questions

- Communication—selection of appropriate medium, clarity of material, quality of product presented, ability to respond to questions

- Content—accuracy, depth, vocabulary, level of understanding

Tier 1 Task (designed to provide evidence of proficient achievement at grade level): The teacher provides a list of possible diseases to be researched. (Alternatively, students may select their own disease to research.) The teacher provides a list of presentation methods as examples, including written report, oral report, and PowerPoint presentation. Students are provided with templates that guide them through the research process, as well as templates relating to each of the presentation methods. Students work in pairs, assigned by the teacher, to support each other as they conduct research, organize their findings, and prepare their presentations.

Tier 2 Task (designed to provide an additional level of challenge): Students work as a group to brainstorm the range of diseases they will research, all possible sources of information, and the range of media they will use to communicate their findings. They will serve as resources for each other throughout the project, collaborating as necessary to accomplish the task.

Tier 3 Task (scaffolded task designed to provide struggling students with an appropriate level of challenge): Students work under the direct supervision of the teacher. Using one disease, the teacher works closely with students to model each step in the research process. Following each modeled step, she has students complete the same step independently, using a second disease that she has selected. She repeats the same modeling/independent work process for each step in the preparation of students' presentations. The presentation medium is tailored to each student's profile.

Figure 8.1: Tiered assignment for grade 5 life science strand on the human body.

The Tier 1 task represents the expected degree of autonomy to be demonstrated by students in grade 5. Specifically, the teacher provides suggestions and templates to guide the students toward success; she also pairs students strategically so they will be able to support each other during the research process. In other words, given the complexity of this task for students in grade 5, she does *not* expect them to demonstrate independence at this time. Depending on the state or provincial curriculum, independent completion of a similar task may be an expectation by the end of the grade 5 year, or perhaps by the end of grade 6. The examination of such expectations must occur as grade teams, school teams, and district teams engage in the curriculum mapping process.

The Tier 2 task allows for a high degree of student autonomy, while at the same time encouraging high-achieving students in the class to act as resources for each other throughout the learning process. The message is "Go for it!" The teacher's role is to monitor and guide, not to teach and direct.

The Tier 3 task recognizes the group of students in Helen's class who require significant supervision. In this version of the task, Helen works closely with students, reviewing content, modeling each step of the research process, and then requiring students to replicate each step. Helen limits choice and provides plenty of structure, while always encouraging students to assume greater responsibility.

Let's now apply the three questions and suggestions that I posed earlier to Helen's tiered task:

1. What essential learning do you intend to assess through this task, regardless of which option students chose? *Common learning targets are identified for all versions of the task.*

2. What common assessment criteria will be applied to each of the choices to ensure consistency with respect to the evidence of learning demonstrated? *Common assessment criteria and the same rubric are used to assess all versions of the task.*

3. Are students always permitted to choose their preferred task—the one that aligns with their strongest learning modality? *Helen relies upon all the data she has gathered about her students—achievement data, anecdotal records detailing strengths and needs, and learner profiles—to guide them toward the appropriate tier.*

In the example that follows (fig. 8.2) Nanci's senior English class is reading and responding to the short story "The Story of an Hour." (This story can be downloaded at **go.solution-tree.com/instruction** and found in reproducible form in the appendix, page 176). The learning targets for all students in the class are the same:

- To improve inferencing skills when reading a short work of fiction
- To communicate complex ideas in a polished presentation

Notice how Nanci:

- Assesses students' initial response to the story
- Sends readers back to the story to find evidence for their responses
- Groups students according to their understanding of the story
- Addresses the same essential learning targets through all choices of assigned tasks
- Uses the same rubric to assess all of the tasks
- Derives the criteria on the rubric from the learning target

---

Nanci's Senior English Lesson

Independent Work

Students receive a copy of the story and the following task to complete:

1. Read the story and immediately write about or tape record the impact it has on you.
2. Reread or relisten to what you have written or said, and analyze how and why the story works.
3. Write or record your thoughts.
4. Write or record a list of questions you have about any aspect of the story.
5. Write or record a summary of what you remember of the facts given by the author: setting, characters, events, and so on.
6. Reread the story using a T-chart to list the details you noted that are actually in the story and those that you added on your own. Based on this exercise, add to your initial analysis of how the story works.

Whole Class and Group Work

Ask students to give a thumbs up, down, or across response to the story: thumbs up means they understood it fully, thumbs down means they didn't understand it, and thumbs across indicates partial understanding.

Gather the thumbs-down and thumbs-across students into small groups, and have the thumbs-up students work together in small groups. Ask students to go over the questions they generated in Step 4 and come up with answers for them. The teacher works with the thumbs-down and -across groups to give more support where needed.

The teacher addresses with the whole class unanswered questions that remain at the conclusion of the group work.

Figure 8.2: Nanci's differentiated lesson for "The Story of an Hour."

continued →

The teacher then assigns the following task:

1. Record or write notes concerning what you have assumed about the characters' personalities, the nature of their relationship, and the life they had together. Make sure you pinpoint exactly what the author wrote that caused you to make each assumption.

2. Collect the students' written or reworded independent analysis of the story.

3. Give out the assignment sheet and the rubric.

4. Using evidence from the collected work, the teacher assesses students' reading performance using the holistic rubric, starting with the thumbs-down group's responses. As students work on the assignment in class, the teacher conducts individual conferences with students who are struggling and negotiates appropriate assignment choices.

Assignment

Choose one of the following:

- Bring one of the two main characters to life in a dramatic interior monologue. Dress the part and speak about the characters' relationship and life together. Use details provided and your own assumptions, but be prepared to use the written text to demonstrate how you arrived at the assumptions during a question and answer follow-up to the monologue.

- Write and perform a dramatization of a scene between the husband and wife that precedes the hour of the story. Communicate to your audience what their life together was like and what each character's personality was like.

- Write an interior monologue from the husband's point of view after the end of the story.

- Write a convincing argument to prove that the story, even though less than two pages long, is as good as a long short story.

- Teach the rest of the class, using a PowerPoint presentation, what can be learned about writing short stories, based on Kate Chopin's "The Story of an Hour."

Source: Nanci Wakeman. Used with permission.

Note that all five assignment choices will provide evidence of the essential learning targets: to improve inferencing skills when reading a short work of fiction and to communicate complex ideas in a polished presentation.

Assessing Essential Learning

In "The Machine Stops" example at the beginning of this chapter, it was unclear what essential learning students were expected to acquire as a result of reading the short story. Without clear learning targets in place, any assessment task will do! But for meaningful and significant learning to occur, teaching and assessment must be purposeful. Granted, at times the learning target in English class may simply be "students will read for enjoyment." And the corresponding assessment task may simply be students sharing with the teacher and their peers what they selected to read and what contributed to their enjoyment. However, typically in a senior literature class, the learning target would involve critical thinking, an understanding of the literature of a particular culture, and so on.

With essential learning targets in place, the teacher considers what range of assessment tasks may be offered to students, with each task designed to provide evidence of the essential learning.

Common Assessment Criteria

Although Nanci's lesson is differentiated, each of the assignment choices will provide evidence of students' inferencing skills. The creation of a common rubric for all of the tasks ensures consistency of the learning evidence that is gathered, regardless of the choice each student makes.

The assessment criteria common to all assignment choices for "The Story of an Hour" are:

- Impact of the presentation (polish, proficiency with chosen medium)

- Communication of interpretation of the story

Figure 8.3 shows the complete rubric used to assess all assignment choices.

Level 1	Level 2	Level 3	Level 4
Presentation is minimally effective and minimally persuasive. Organization is faulty, and the medium is used with limited craftsmanship. Student presents little accurate content and an unsophisticated interpretation of the story.	Presentation is effective and persuasive to some degree. Use of medium is organized and crafted to some degree. Student presents partially accurate content and some insightful interpretation of the story.	Presentation is effective and persuasive. Use of the medium is organized and well crafted. Student presents accurate and apt content and an insightful interpretation of the story.	Presentation is effective, novel, and persuasive. Use of the medium is organized, well crafted, and fluid. Student presents accurate and apt content and an insightful, expert interpretation of the story.

Figure 8.3: Holistic rubric for assessing "The Story of an Hour" presentations.

By contrast to the grade 5 tiered science task, this senior English example allows for a much greater degree of student choice. The students in Nanci's class are mature high school students and demonstrate much less variation in skills than Helen's students. Nevertheless, there are students in this class who struggle to make inferences from text—hence the need to differentiate the learning process that precedes the final assignment.

Moving Students Out of Their Comfort Zone

I frequently visit classrooms in which the teacher has embraced Gardner's multiple intelligences research and used a variety of interest and aptitude surveys to identify learning modalities. Students spend most of their time working comfortably within their preferred modality. By contrast, the effective teacher coaches and challenges students so that they are working within their preferred modality sometimes, while at other times they are challenged to demonstrate learning in less comfortable modes.

Skilled, sensitive teachers who are attuned to the strengths and needs of all of their students appear to be able to do this intuitively. This is yet another example of professional judgment. Such judgment requires constant monitoring and adjustment on the part of the teacher, not only with respect to a student's knowledge and skill levels, but also, and perhaps more importantly, with respect to the student's emotional well-being. Just like adults, students are better able to undertake challenging work when their confidence level is high. At such times, it is appropriate to nudge a student toward a challenge. When the confidence of a child who prefers to draw or to create a mind map is high, I may suggest she undertake a written task.

Balanced Assessment: Write, Do, and Say

There are two reasons why a balance of written, performance, and oral assessment evidence is necessary: first, not all students are able to demonstrate what they have learned if they only have opportunities to write about their learning. (I say *write* because it tends to be the default assessment option for many teachers, especially in the middle and high school grades). Second, many of the learning outcomes appearing in curriculum documents demand assessment through *doing* and *saying*. While performance tasks are an integral part of the assessment process in performance disciplines such as physical education and instrumental music and oral assessment is common in modern languages, all disciplines contain important learning targets that may be validly assessed only through performance or the spoken word.

I frequently hear from teachers about the poor expressive language skills of their students. As we chat, it often becomes clear that writing takes precedence over oral language in their programs. Yet talking is essential to develop thinking skills, vocabulary power, and confidence in children and young adults. This is especially true for boys. In my years working with at-risk students, I would frequently say, "Notebooks and pens away! It's time to talk!" I can still hear the cheers in response to this instruction. If our goal is to improve young students' skills in responding to literature, then we are well advised to provide numerous opportunities for them to talk—and listen—to each other. Here is an example of powerful talk, taken from my own teaching experience.

The Poetry Response Circle

Many years ago, when teaching high school English, I used a "response to poetry" model to engage my students in thoughtful examination of poetry. Like my colleagues, I found that many students didn't like poetry, often because they couldn't get the hang of understanding things that weren't actually written in the text! Of course, each of my classes also included a handful of students who *were* able to read between the lines, respond to imagery, and discern what the poet was saying. This response to poetry model drew on the "reciprocal teaching" approach (Sullivan Palincsar & Brown, 1984), which activates students as resources to support and build on each other's learning.

Depending on the length of the poem, I may have asked students to read it the night before. For shorter poems, this wasn't necessary. Students moved their desks into one large circle for the first few times we did this, or once the class had become familiar with the routine, into three circles, with one-third of the students in each circle.

We would read the poem together, and if the poem was short, we might read it a second time. Students would then be invited to comment on the poem, perhaps making a personal connection or giving an evaluative comment.

In senior classes where students were more confident, comments were more freewheeling, and I would occasionally ask a particular student to add to the discussion if he or she had been quiet. With less competent or confident students, I would employ a more structured approach. For example, during each go-round, each student would offer a comment, with the expectation that every student would participate but had the option of "passing" twice during the session. Further structure was sometimes necessary, with the first go-round simply requiring students to comment on whether they liked or disliked the poem. On the next go-round, I might ask them to identify a word or line they didn't understand, and then invite anyone in the circle to offer a meaning or interpretation.

The great strength of the poetry circle is that students lacking in confidence and interpretive skills benefit from hearing what their peers have to say. When configured in the large circle, I can intervene as much or as little as necessary to keep discussion flowing and to sensitively draw reluctant students into the discussion. When utilizing three circles functioning simultaneously, I ensure that each circle contains a vacant chair, so that I am able to join any of the circles at any time. The response to poetry circle is a highly effective structure for differentiating the assessment of students' oral skills. (Of course, this same structure may be applied in other subjects.)

How did I assess students' communication skills during poetry circle? Depending on my intended focus for assessment, I would select either a rubric to assess their reading skills or, if my intent was to assess their listening and speaking skills, a rubric similar to the one in figure 8.4. (Visit **go.solution-tree .com/instruction** to find the complete version of the informal speaking and listening rubric.) In either case, I would sample performance, both with respect to the number of students I was observing during a given poetry circle and by assessing only selected criteria from the rubric. That is, on any given day, I would assess only some of my students, with respect to selected criteria from the rubric. Over time, I would assess every student, several times, with respect to all criteria. All of these decisions were purposeful with respect to my overall assessment plan for the class. Hence, assessment could be diagnostic, formative, or summative. In the case of summative assessment, I would ensure that I had sufficient data for each student to draw reliable conclusions about their listening and speaking skills for grading and reporting purposes.

Assessment Tools That Encourage Learning

While rubrics are vital tools in communicating to students the performance standards we expect them to meet, there is a danger that some students may be discouraged by standards they believe to be unattainable. Here again, the teacher's professional judgment must come into play to ensure that students are presented with performance goals they perceive as challenging but achievable—in other words, goals that are within their zone of proximal development.

One way to accomplish this is to develop checklists, designed for self- and peer assessment, based on whichever level of a given rubric represents an achievable challenge for a given group. Figure 8.5 (page 118) presents part of a generic rubric for assessing research skills. See **go.solution-tree.com /instruction** for the complete rubric. The checklist in figure 8.6 is based on the Level 4 indicators on the rubric, representing exemplary research skills, and would be appropriate for students deemed ready to demonstrate skills at this level.

Name: _____ Date: _____

Categories/ Criteria	Level 1	Level 2	Level 3	Level 4
Thinking	Demonstrates limited ability to explore/express thoughts when speaking to others	Demonstrates some ability to explore/express thoughts when speaking to others (e.g., is beginning to reflect, analyze, hypothesize)	Explores/ expresses own thoughts when speaking to others (e.g., reflects, analyzes, hypothesizes)	Explores/ expresses original/ creative thoughts when speaking to others (e.g., reflects, analyzes, hypothesizes)
	Demonstrates limited ability to build on the ideas of others	Demonstrates some ability to build on the ideas of others	Builds on the ideas of others when speaking	Integrates and extends the ideas of others when speaking
Communi-cation	Expresses ideas, opinions, and feelings with limited clarity when speaking to others in terms of: • Fluency • Volume • Speed • Intonation • Inflection	Expresses ideas, opinions, and feelings with partial clarity when speaking to others in terms of: • Fluency • Volume • Speed • Intonation • Inflection	Expresses ideas, opinions, and feelings clearly when speaking to others in terms of: • Fluency • Volume • Speed • Intonation • Inflection	Expresses ideas, opinions, and feelings clearly and in an engaging manner when speaking to others in terms of: • Fluency • Volume • Speed • Intonation • Inflection
	Uses a limited vocabulary	Attempts to use new vocabulary	Uses new vocabulary effectively	Explores new vocabulary successfully
	Has difficulty maintaining appropriate eye contact when speaking	Maintains eye contact some of the time when speaking	Maintains appropriate eye contact when speaking	Establishes and maintains eye contact when speaking
	Makes limited use of gestures when speaking	Makes some use of gestures when speaking	Uses gestures effectively when speaking	Uses gestures naturally and effectively when speaking
Active Listening	Demonstrates limited ability to listen to others' ideas, opinions, points of view	Listens some of the time to others' ideas, opinions, points of view	Listens attentively to others' ideas, opinions, points of view	Listens attentively and respectfully to others' ideas, opinions, points of view
	Challenges to others' ideas, opinions, points of view may be inappropriate	Attempts to challenge others' ideas, opinions, points of view appropriately	Challenges others' ideas, opinions, points of view appropriately	Challenges others' ideas, opinions, points of view appropriately and constructively

From Cooper. Talk About Assessment, *1E. © 2006 Nelson Education Ltd. Reproduced by permission.* www.cengage.com/permissions

Figure 8.4: Informal speaking and listening rubric.

Note: Use this rubric to observe individual students and/or groups of students as they are engaged in the research process (for example, as they work in the library, or during a one-on-one conference).

Categories/ Criteria	Level 1	Level 2	Level 3	Level 4
Focusing	Has difficulty formulating appropriate questions to guide research	Formulates simple questions to guide research	Formulates appropriate questions to guide research	Formulates insightful questions to guide research
Surveying Sources of Information	Considers only a limited number of sources	Considers a narrow range of primary and/or secondary sources	Considers a wide range of appropriate primary and/or secondary sources	Considers a full range of the most appropriate primary and/or secondary sources
Formulating a Question	• Has difficulty formulating a workable research question • Has difficulty revising or is reluctant to revise question	• Formulates a simple research question • Shows some ability to revise question, as necessary, according to results of research	• Formulates a workable research question • Revises question, as necessary, according to results of research	• Formulates an insightful and workable research question • Revises question in insightful ways, according to results of research
Researching	• Locates a limited number of sources • Has difficulty making appropriate selections based on 　+ Relevance to topic 　+ Reliability 　+ Variety of perspective 　+ Degree of bias • Demonstrates limited ability to record information in a systematic way	• Locates a narrow range of primary and/or secondary sources • Demonstrates some ability to make appropriate selections based on 　+ Relevance to topic 　+ Reliability 　+ Variety of perspective 　+ Degree of bias • Demonstrates some ability to record information in a systematic way	• Locates a wide range of primary and/or secondary sources • Makes appropriate selections based on 　+ Relevance to topic 　+ Reliability 　+ Variety of perspective 　+ Degree of bias • Records information in a systematic way	• Locates a full range of the most appropriate primary and/or secondary sources • Makes the most appropriate selections based on 　+ Relevance to topic 　+ Reliability 　+ Variety of perspective 　+ Degree of bias • Routinely records information in a systematic way

From Cooper. Talk About Assessment HS Flyer 2009-10. *© 2010 Nelson Education Ltd. Reproduced by permission. www.cengage.com/permissions*

Figure 8.5: The research process rubric.

Research Process Checklist										

Name: _____ **Term:** _____

Record the date each time you use this checklist.
Make a check mark under the date when you are able to reply "Yes" to the question.

	Date									
Have I asked appropriate questions to guide my research?										
Have I considered a wide range of appropriate primary and/or secondary sources?										
Have I produced a workable research question?										
Have I revised my research question, as necessary, according to results of my research?										
Have I located a wide range of appropriate primary and/or secondary sources?										
Have I made appropriate selections of sources based on relevance to topic, reliability, and variety of perspectives/degree of bias?										
Have I recorded the information in a systematic way?										
Have I recorded the sources of all information?										
Have I classified or categorized the information appropriately and effectively?										
Have I created notes and graphic organizers to represent the information effectively?										
Have I synthesized and evaluated my findings with accuracy?										
Have I formulated a thesis statement that answers my research question?										
Have I identified sufficient supporting evidence to explain and defend my thesis?										
Summary of things I need to work on										

From Talk About Assessment HS Flyer 2009–2010. © 2010 Nelson Education Ltd. Reproduced by permission. www.cengage.com/permissions

Figure 8.6: Checklist for students with exemplary research skills.

The second checklist (fig. 8.7) is based on the indicators for Level 1 on the research process rubric and would be appropriate for students who are experiencing significant difficulty with respect to these skills. Compare the complexity of skills expected of students on this tool to those on the original checklist (page 119).

Adapted Research Process Checklist	Date										
Self-Assessment Questions											
Do I have a question to guide my research?											
Do I have at least two sources?											
Am I able to explain how my sources will help to answer my question?											
Am I able to show how I will record information from my sources?											
Do I have headings for organizing my information?											
Have I created notes in my own words to summarize the information under each heading?											
Have I formed my own opinion about the information I have gathered?											
Have I answered my research question?											
Am I prepared to answer questions about my research and my conclusions?											

Name: _____ Term: _____

Record the date each time you use this checklist. Make a check mark under the date when you are able to reply "Yes" to the question.

Things I need to work on

Figure 8.7: Checklist for students having difficulty with research skills.

As struggling students begin to master the skills associated with this task, the adapted checklist may be replaced by the regular research process checklist.

In chapter 7 (page 89), teachers adjusted their instruction according to students' zone of proximal development. The same principle applies where the focus is assessment. In fact, when teachers come to realize that the most effective assessment strategies are indistinguishable from instruction, they have understood the concept of informative assessment. In classrooms that are increasingly populated by students demonstrating an ever-wider range of ability, such understanding is crucial.

Conclusion

The effective differentiated class provides students with a menu tailored to their needs; they are not invited to a buffet to gorge on their dish of choice. Responsive teachers take the time to develop profiles of their students by drawing upon a rich variety of data and anecdotal information. When designing assessments that will improve learning as well as measure it, these teachers use this deep knowledge of their students to create tasks that are adapted to those profiles. In other words, they design their assessments with their students in mind.

Proactive planning ensures that tasks are differentiated appropriately, that is, that they are designed to present all students with tasks that are challenging but not frustrating. Tiering is one strategy that facilitates such planning. Tiering can help teachers ensure that while different versions of a task may vary in complexity according to student differences, all versions of the task will provide evidence of the same essential learnings. While tiering can help to ensure that all students are working within their zone of proximal development, teachers must avoid the trap of ability-grouping. Students' levels of skill and understanding will naturally vary according to a given task. Such variation may be attributable to differing levels of interest in a topic, growing confidence, factors at home, and so on. Hence, while a student may need to work on a less complex version of a task in a civics unit, she may be able to handle a complex, open-ended science task.

Effective differentiation requires the teacher to constantly monitor students' proficiency and adjust the complexity of the assessment task accordingly. This may mean that a teacher needs to nudge students out of their comfort zone to undertake work that is more challenging. There is a dangerous myth that prevails in many special education settings: "Struggling students learn most effectively when tasks are simple and broken down into very small steps." This can lead to work that is easy, mindless, and irrelevant. In my experience, students are not looking for work to be easy; they are looking for work that is engaging.

Responsive teachers who work with at-risk and struggling learners understand that of the many ways students may demonstrate their learning, writing is usually the most difficult. All too often, these students face double jeopardy: they are struggling to understand new content and, at the same time, struggling to express themselves through writing. Effective assessment plans include an appropriate balance of oral, written, and performance evidence, according to the learning targets to be assessed and the range of student characteristics. Highly skilled teachers carefully examine learning outcome statements to see whether they specify that students *must* communicate their understanding through writing, or as is usually the case, whether content knowledge may be demonstrated through any communication mode. Highly skilled teachers are also skeptical before concluding, based on written evidence alone, that a student does not understand a concept. These teachers will sit beside the student and ask him or her to demonstrate their understanding using manipulatives, or perhaps by drawing an image. Let us remind ourselves that assessment work is detective work: conclusions must be based on sufficient evidence drawn from multiple sources.

CHAPTER 9

How Do I Grade Learning in the Mixed-Ability Class?

In this chapter I use the terms *grade* and *grading*, as Ken O'Connor (2009) does, to refer to the periodic summarizing of learning for the purpose of reporting growth, progress, or achievement to students and parents.

A teacher approached me at the end of a recent workshop and made the following observation:

> I feel so badly for lots of my kids. They come into my class at the beginning of the year with so many gaps in their learning. They work really hard and make all kinds of progress. But then when they get their report cards, they get Cs or Ds. It just doesn't seem fair. Any suggestions?

The concern voiced by this teacher is all too prevalent in today's standards-based classrooms. Students who struggle will see little point in working diligently if the consequence at grading time is a symbol that represents "limited achievement." Here was my response:

> This is a common occurrence in standards-based systems where the standard for excellence is often set quite arbitrarily, and the same standard is applied to all. I'm sure that, as well as the students you just described, you have others who came into and left your class getting As. They didn't have to work particularly hard, and, based on their grades, they appear to have made no progress—because there was none to be made! This situation occurs when grades reflect only achievement, at a given moment in time, according to preset performance standards. The students you describe need recognition of the progress that has occurred, measured from your preinstruction to your postinstruction assessment data. If your school or district's grading and reporting system measures only achievement, then create

your own system to recognize the progress that students have made. For example, prior to the release of official report cards, celebrate as a class the gains made by your students. Develop your own ways, or even better, have your students suggest how to recognize and celebrate their accomplishments.

Michael Fullan (Fullan, Hill, & Crévola, 2006) describes how the "factory model" of schooling fails to serve students with differing strengths and needs:

> Students are grouped into grades, based primarily on age rather than readiness to learn . . . . The grade progression model is a factory assembly-line model of schooling that assumes equal readiness to learn and equal rates of learning . . . . The model makes assessment of students to establish starting points irrelevant because the starting points are dictated by the curriculum, not by the readiness of students to learn. (p. 31)

For teachers to be able to counter these potentially destructive consequences of grading and reporting protocols, they need to understand the differences between the following types of grading systems:

- Norm-referenced grading—grades that compare one student's achievement to the achievement of other students

- Criterion-referenced grading—grades that are based on a prescribed set of performance standards

- Self-referenced grading—grades that compare a student's recent achievement with that student's earlier achievement, often with reference to a growth continuum

In determining which system to use when, educators need to be aware of the difference between *growth, progress,* and *achievement.* Growth is a measure of the increase in student learning that has occurred over time, compared to baseline data; progress is a measure of the improvement that has occurred from a baseline toward a specified performance standard; and achievement is a measure of what a student knows or can do at a given point in time.

When to Use Norm-Referenced Grading

Historically, norm-referenced grading systems have been used to sift and sort students into high-, average-, and low-achieving groups.

Norm-referenced grading is often used when the purpose of the grading process is to select a small number of students for entrance into a particular program or institution. Because the reference point is the achievement of other students, norm-referenced systems allow the standards to be adjusted after an assessment has occurred. Unfortunately, norm-referenced practices often lead to the rules being changed long after the game has been played. My son, who recently completed a four-year degree program, would occasionally celebrate his achievement on a midterm test, only to learn days later that the results were "bell-curved" (fig. 9.1), and his grade of B had now changed to a C.

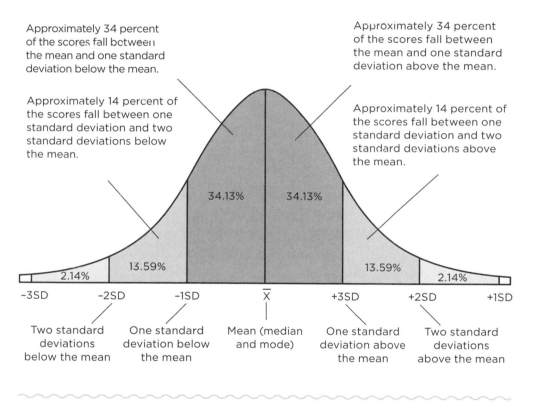

Approximately 34 percent of the scores fall between the mean and one standard deviation below the mean.

Approximately 14 percent of the scores fall between one standard deviation and two standard deviations below the mean.

Approximately 34 percent of the scores fall between the mean and one standard deviation above the mean.

Approximately 14 percent of the scores fall between one standard deviation and two standard deviations above the mean.

34.13%   34.13%

2.14%   13.59%   13.59%   2.14%

−3SD   −2SD   −1SD $\overline{X}$ +3SD   +2SD   +1SD

Two standard deviations below the mean

One standard deviation below the mean

Mean (median and mode)

One standard deviation above the mean

Two standard deviations above the mean

Figure 9.1: The normal curve.

Adherence to norm-referenced grading tends to reinforce certain beliefs and leads to a number of questionable practices (fig. 9.2, page 126). And while norm-referenced grading continues to prevail in postsecondary institutions, grading experts are unanimous in deeming it inappropriate for kindergarten to grade 12 (Guskey, 2006; O'Connor, 2011; Reeves, 2007).

Norm-Referenced Beliefs	Norm-Referenced Practices
Intelligence is fixed and distributed normally.	When grading, I expect only a few students to receive As, many to receive Bs and Cs, and a few to receive Ds and Fs.
Socioeconomic status, family background, and other out-of-school variables outweigh the impact of teaching in determining achievement.	I do not expect the same amount of learning or quality of work from those students who come from poorer backgrounds.
My best students and my weakest students define the range of achievement in my class.	What I expect in terms of quality from my students will vary from year to year, depending on whether I have a strong class or a weak class.
My job is to cover the curriculum.	I do not adjust my teaching to meet the differing needs of some students.
Many important criteria for learning cannot be defined, for example, creativity.	I do not provide rubrics or share work samples with students. I know quality when I see it.

Figure 9.2: Norm-referenced beliefs and practices.

When to Use Criterion-Referenced Grading

Criterion-referenced grading is common in standards-based systems wherein teachers use rubrics to communicate to students the levels of performance associated with a set of grades. Criterion-referencing is appropriate and necessary when the goal is to certify students as having met a prescribed level of knowledge or proficiency on a specified set of learning targets. Hence, skill-based curricula, such as driving a car or music certification, utilize criterion-referenced grading. The sample of level descriptions in figure 9.3 is an excerpt from the national music curriculum in the United Kingdom.

Level 3

Pupils recognize and explore the ways sounds can be combined and used expressively. They sing in tune with expression and perform rhythmically simple parts that use a limited range of notes. They improvise repeated patterns and combine several layers of sound with awareness of the combined effect. They recognize how the different musical elements are combined and used expressively and make improvements to their own work, commenting on the intended effect.

Level 4

Pupils identify and explore the relationship between sounds and how music reflects different intentions. While performing by ear and from simple notations, they maintain their own part with awareness of how the different parts fit together and the need to achieve an overall effect. They improvise melodic and rhythmic phrases as part of a group performance and compose by developing ideas within musical structures. They describe, compare and evaluate different kinds of music using an appropriate musical vocabulary. They suggest improvements to their own and others' work, commenting on how intentions have been achieved.

Level 5

Pupils identify and explore musical devices and how music reflects time, place and culture. They perform significant parts from memory and from notations, with awareness of their own contribution such as leading others, taking a solo part or providing rhythmic support. They improvise melodic and rhythmic material within given structures, use a variety of notations, and compose music for different occasions using appropriate musical devices. They analyze and compare musical features. They evaluate how venue, occasion and purpose affect the way music is created, performed and heard. They refine and improve their work.

Source: Department for Education, United Kingdom. Reprinted with permission.

Figure 9.3. Skill-level descriptions for music, United Kingdom.

The rubric in figure 9.4 (page 128) is a school-developed, classroom assessment tool based on these national music standards. The rubric serves as a clear, easy-to-use set of performance standards to guide students toward the expected level of musical proficiency. It may be used by students themselves for peer assessment during the learning process and by the teacher for diagnostic, formative, and summative assessment purposes. The music rubric may be downloaded at **go.solution-tree.com/instruction** and found in the appendix (page 180).

Name:			Form:		
Level 3			**Unit**	**Date**	**Sig.**
	Sing in tune with expression.				
	Perform simple melodies or rhythms.				
	Improvise repeated patterns.				
	Combine layers of sound with awareness of the effect.				
	Recognize how the different musical elements are combined and used expressively.				
	Make improvements to my own work.				
Level 4			**Unit**	**Date**	**Sig.**
	Perform from simple notations.				
	Maintain my own part with awareness of others.				
	Improvise melodies and rhythms.				
	Compose using musical shapes.				
	Describe, compare, and discuss different kinds of music using musical vocabulary.				
	Suggest improvements to my own work and others' work.				
Level 5			**Unit**	**Date**	**Sig.**
	Perform parts from memory and notations, for example, taking a solo part and/or providing rhythms.				
	Improvise melodies and rhythms within given structures.				
	Compose music for different occasions using a variety of notations.				
	Evaluate how venue, occasion, and purpose affect the way music is created, performed, and heard.				
	Refine and improve my work.				

Source: Walkden High School, Worsley, Manchester, United Kingdom.

Figure 9.4: Music rubric from Walkden High School, U.K., for 11-to-14 year olds.

As school districts across the United States and Canada implement standards-based approaches to curriculum, assessment, and grading in which the goal is proficiency for *all* students, they must make the shift from norm-referenced grading, in which achievement is measured relative to other students, to criterion-referenced grading, where performance standards are preestablished, public, and consistent.

When to Use Self-Referenced Grading

A self-referenced grading system is necessary and appropriate when describing the learning of students at risk, as well as when describing young children's acquisition of essential skill sets such as reading, speaking, and writing. Self-referenced grading is most effective when it is referenced to a growth continuum—a research-based description of the stages that learners typically pass through as they develop fluency in a set of target skills. In this case, the term *grading* is in fact a misnomer, because self-referenced grading, relative to a growth continuum, provides descriptive, not numerical or letter grade information, to parents and students. When linked to a growth continuum, self-referenced grading also provides teachers with performance indicators that enable them to differentiate instruction. Consider, for example, the excerpt from the kindergarten literacy continuum in figure 9.5 (page 130). Visit **go.solution-tree.com /instruction** for the complete continuum.

Self-referenced grading is crucial when working with struggling students, because it measures growth from a preinstruction baseline, wherever that may be for individual students. At reporting time, there are no failing grades that may discourage students and their parents; rather, students and their parents receive descriptive information about current skill levels, relative to where students began, as well as information about the next level to be demonstrated.

What Are the Attributes of High-Quality Grades?

Regardless of the reference point for grades, teachers must ensure that the grades they employ to summarize students' learning meet stringent standards of quality. Ken O'Connor identifies four essential attributes for quality grades: grades should be meaningful, consistent, accurate, and supportive of learning (Cooper & O'Connor, 2008).

Developmental Aspects	Emerging With Direct Support . . . ➡	Developing With Guided Support . . . ➡	Applying With Minimal Support . . . ➡	Extending ➡
The Child	May draw on personal connections while participating in a variety of reading/viewing experiences to make meaning.	Draws on and begins to develop strategies (e.g., making connections, predicting, asking questions, and reflecting) while participating in a variety of reading/viewing experiences to make meaning.	Draws on and expands strategies (e.g., making connections, predicting, asking questions, and reflecting) while participating in a variety of reading/viewing experiences to make meaning.	Draws on, expands, and begins to identify strategies (e.g., making connections, predicting, asking questions, and reflecting) while participating in a variety of reading/viewing experiences to make meaning.
Thinking/Metacognition				
Developing dispositions— awareness, attention, interest, participation, curiosity, engagement, perseverance	With direct support may attend to and may participate in reading/viewing activities (e.g., makes meaning from text using pictures, pattern, memory, prior knowledge).	With guided support engages in reading/viewing activities (e.g., makes meaning from text using pictures, pattern, memory, prior knowledge).	With minimal support purposefully engages in reading/viewing activities (e.g., makes meaning from text using pictures, pattern, memory, prior knowledge).	Purposefully engages in reading/viewing activities (e.g., makes meaning from text using emergent reading strategies).
Setting purpose—	With direct support may participate in setting purpose for reading/viewing.	With guided support sets a purpose for reading/viewing.	With minimal support chooses a purpose for reading/viewing.	Identifies a purpose for reading/viewing; participates in the reading/viewing process.
Processing—	With direct support may express some thoughts and understanding before/during and after reading/viewing (may be unrelated to topic).	With guided support expresses some thoughts and understanding before/during and after reading/viewing.	With minimal support expresses thoughts and understanding before/during and after reading/viewing.	Expresses thoughts and understanding before/during and after reading/viewing.

*A variety of teacher, peer, and environmental supports can be provided at any stage of development.

Source: Kindergarten Learning Project *(2008). Grateful acknowledgment to the Kindergarten Learning Project Team, the British Columbia Ministry of Education, and Qualicum British Columbia School District 69. Reprinted with permission.*

Figure 9.5: Kindergarten emergent literacy continuum: reading and viewing.

Grades Should Be Meaningful

Grades must meaningfully represent a student's achievement of learning outcomes. "A single summary symbol may not provide a clear enough description of achievement. Organizing assessment information by learning outcome enables teachers to produce a profile of strengths and areas for improvement" (Cooper & O'Connor, 2008, p. 24).

As we saw in the grade 10 mathematics case study in chapter 1 (page 16), passing grades as low as 50 percent often carry little meaning with respect to the knowledge and skills mastered by students. Jeff Catania, a colleague and a consultant in mathematics and science, recently observed:

> What I have found overwhelmingly (from my recent work in looking at a developmental continuum in math and diagnostic assessment thereof) is that an alarming number of students (one-half or more in some grades) have little or no conceptual understanding of the mathematics they are being taught. Math students have become excellent mimics of procedures, and we accept that as "learning" even though they have major gaps in their understanding that reach back multiple grades in many cases. (J. Catania, personal communication, March 30, 2010)

The passing grades that these students receive each year in mathematics are certainly *not* meaningful. Although the grades are interpreted to mean that students are minimally proficient and therefore ready to move to the next grade level, this is not the case. While passing grades as low as 50 percent enable students to move from elementary school to middle school, from middle school to high school, and even to graduate, they are usually invalid measures of proficiency, having typically been raised from grades in the high forties. Such grades are also dishonest, and harmful, since they set students up for failure at the next grade level.

The work of the mathematics department chairs described in chapter 1 is ground-breaking. Accepting the fact that 50 percent will continue to be the pass/fail cut point, they are redesigning all mathematics assessments, as well as revising grading practices, to be able to assure students and their parents that a final grade of 50 percent indicates a minimal level of proficiency on *all* essential learning outcomes.

This example serves as a blueprint for teachers working collaboratively to ensure that the grades students receive are meaningful. Teachers of other subject areas may wish to review the case study in chapter 1 and consider how the process undertaken by the mathematics chairs might be applied to their own subject domain.

Grades Should Be Consistent

Grades must be consistent—that is, the same performance by a student should result in the same grade even when it is from different teachers of the same subject or grade level. "To achieve consistency, educators need to ensure they are working from a common understanding of learning outcomes and performance standards" (Cooper & O'Connor, 2008, p. 24).

When I ask workshop participants to identify their major concerns with respect to assessment and grading, lack of consistency is always high on the list. However, while educators are quick to identify this as a problem, few know how to address it. Here are my recommendations to improve consistency in both assessment and grading:

- Commit to meeting regularly with colleagues to talk about assessment and grading practices and procedures.

- Where they exist, review state, provincial, district, and school performance standards.

- Working with grade-level or course colleagues, commit to the development of common assessment tasks and corresponding assessment tools such as rubrics, checklists, and scoring guides.

- Administer common assessments to students and participate in common (moderated) grading sessions. Use these sessions to refine the design of assessment tasks and tools and to select anchors (student work samples) that are aligned with the assessment tools you have developed.

- Frequently examine your own and your school's methods for summarizing sets of student marks into summary grades, and discuss levels of consistency.

- Read professional materials (texts, journals, online resources) to stay abreast of research.

While grading is not, strictly speaking, part of the teaching/learning process, it is arguably the most public function that teachers perform. As such, educators have a commitment to students, parents, and themselves to ensure that grading beliefs, practices, and procedures can withstand the most rigorous scrutiny from all stakeholders.

Grades Should Be Accurate

"Grades should be unencumbered by other factors and should be as pure a measure of achievement as possible. Effort, behavior, attitude, and other nonachievement factors should not inflate or deflate the grade" (Cooper & O'Connor, 2008, p. 24).

We saw earlier that norm-referenced grading models summarize student achievement by comparing one student's performance relative to other students. Hence, the standards change from class to class and year to year. On the other hand, criterion-referenced grading is characterized by preestablished, public standards to which all students are expected to aspire. Furthermore, there are no preconceived expectations regarding the numbers of students who will meet the standards; there is a belief in and commitment to excellence for all. It follows that in a criterion-referenced grading system, an A means an *A*. It does not mean "excellent achievement" for some students and "excellent effort, though poor achievement" for others.

Of course, the danger inherent in maintaining clear and consistent performance standards for all students is that struggling students may become discouraged when, despite plenty of hard work, they continually receive poor grades. We address this problem in chapter 10 (page 141). For now, let me point out that, despite teachers' best intentions when inflating grades for struggling students, a true sense of self-esteem does *not* come from a false sense of achievement. In my own teaching career, I have encountered many students who knew, despite having reached high school, that their reading and writing skills were woefully deficient. In short, when grading, teachers must clearly distinguish between achievement and effort.

Grades Should Be Supportive of Learning

"Grading is most supportive of learning when students are involved in the entire learning process. When students know what the goals and criteria for success are, when they know which assessments are part of the instructional process and which assessments will be used as summative indicators of achievement for grading purposes, they are more likely to see the purpose of assessment as learning and not as accumulating grades" (Cooper & O'Connor, 2008, p. 24).

You may recall the story from chapter 6 regarding the struggling, and in some cases, failing students in a grade 10 history class who received their grades as they left the classroom on an otherwise sunny Friday afternoon. As indicated, the low and failing percentage grades were due in most cases to zeroes having been assigned when students did not submit work. How can grades be supportive of learning in this case? In short, they can't! A poor grade will only motivate a student who is used to receiving good grades.

Many students who perpetually receive poor or failing grades eventually give up and drop out of school.

When students do not submit one or more major pieces of work, instead of receiving a grade, they must receive an *incomplete*. The message to the student is "The sample of evidence you have submitted for grading purposes is incomplete, so I am unable to determine a grade." The purpose of this approach is to kick-start a completion plan that will involve the student, teacher, possibly a resource teacher, and possibly a parent.

Principles for Sound and Supportive Grading

Because sound assessment and grading policies provide the foundation for fair and supportive actions by teachers, let us now consider the principles that must inform the grading component of these policies.

1. The purpose of grades and report cards is to provide parents and students with a concise summary of the learning that has occurred within a prescribed instructional period. To be helpful insofar as they contribute to further learning, grades must communicate, simply and effectively, one or more of the following:

    -   **Growth**—how much improvement has occurred, measured forward from baseline data

    -   **Progress**—how far a student has progressed towards an expected standard during an instructional period

    -   **Achievement**—how well a student has performed at a moment in time, referenced to a known standard

2. Grades must be determined using consistent procedures or algorithms. Teachers at all grade levels must collaborate and reach agreement concerning the amount and kinds of evidence that will be used for grading purposes, and they must also agree on how grades, scores, and anecdotal information will be combined into one or more summary grades. Typically, in the early years, the process of summarizing data about student learning into summary grades is unlikely to involve complex arithmetic calculation, because there tends to be less data to summarize; furthermore, decisions about promotion to the next grade level are often less dependent upon specific, administratively set cut points. But these factors do not preclude the need for teachers to agree upon consistent procedures for determining summary grades and

communicating these procedures to parents. Moving into the junior, middle, and senior grades, teachers are more likely to rely upon algorithms and more complex arithmetic computation to determine summary grades. Teachers at these grade levels tend to rely increasingly on grading software to assist in the computation of summary grades. Teachers using such software should know precisely how grades are computed and should be able to explain and justify the use of the software in terms of its consistency with sound grading principles.

3. Grades must represent the best possible summary of a student's learning over time. Most of the distress that occurs at reporting intervals is caused by grades that come as a surprise to students and parents. Any grade that comes as a surprise is a problem grade! Grades should confirm the trend in growth, progress, or achievement that has been observed over time by the teacher and has been communicated, informally, to students and parents, during an instructional period.

   Grades that do not surprise students and parents are also those that provide the best possible summary of learning over the course of an instructional period. This means that grades representing the mode or the median are preferable to grades based on the mean or average.

4. Grades should be weighted more heavily according to a student's best or more recent work. In a related vein to guideline 3, if we assume that instruction is effective and that students are working to improve, it makes sense when determining summary grades to ascribe greater importance to more recently completed work than to early attempts. Using a sports analogy, summary grades should not include marks from tryouts or practices; they should be based on results from regular season games and playoffs, with marks from the playoffs carrying the greater weight.

5. While grading methods should be consistent, teachers must determine grades using a combination of numerical calculation, knowledge of students, and their professional judgment to arrive at grades that are fair and sensitive to each student. Some students may perform poorly under the pressure of the game, or the playoff, despite having been successful in many of the practices. If this occurs, the teacher must exercise professional judgment, rather

than adhering to a rigid procedure for determining the grade. (Professional judgment comprises decisions made by educators, in light of experience, and with reference to shared public standards and established policies and guidelines.) For example, if the teacher has compelling evidence from practice that a student has mastered a particular learning target, then the summary grade should reflect mastery.

While teachers of the same grade or course should collaborate in the identification of the evidence that will be used to determine summary grades, this body of evidence (Wiggins & McTighe, 1998) may differ for some students, according to individual circumstances. Once again, teachers need to recognize the role of professional judgment when making grading decisions for certain students.

6. Grades are, at best, brief summaries of student learning. As such, they are incomplete and do not reveal details about precisely what has been learned and what remains to be learned. More detailed explanations, class records, anecdotal comments, portfolios of work, and face-to-face discussions are necessary to explain the rich information that lies behind each grade. Single summary grades—for example, "Physical Education: 75%"—hold little meaning for students or parents. Standards-based grades, which provide data about essential learning targets, are much more informative. For example:

    Movement skills and concepts: B

    Physical fitness: A

    Health concepts and choices: B

Regardless of the level of detail provided by the formal report card, informal communication is necessary to explain the learning behind the grades. This communication may take the form of email, telephone conversations, notes home, or other such methods. Early communication with parents is critical for struggling students. But while there is a tendency for these communications to occur only when problems arise, good news about improvement or noteworthy achievement is extremely important to building the self-esteem of students and providing parents with a cause for celebration.

7. Measurement error is a naturally occurring, ever-present element of all grading processes. Measurement error occurs because a grade is a single summary score of only a sample of what a student has learned and is determined by one human being (the teacher) when looking at the work of another human being (the student). Grading has much in common with polling. Polling companies make inferences about the voting preferences of a population by identifying a statistically representative sample, determining its preferences through assessment, and then reporting results by extrapolating to the whole population. Grading involves taking a sample of the work students have produced as evidence of their learning, assessing it, and then extrapolating from the sample to draw conclusions about the learning that has occurred within a reporting period. But polling and grading differ in one significant way: polling companies acknowledge and communicate measurement error. They will typically announce, "These results are accurate 19 times out of 20, plus or minus 5 percentage points." Instead of acknowledging that there may be as much as a 5 percent variation between students' grades that is attributable to measurement error, we imply to students and parents that there is *no* measurement error. In fact, we may go so far as to express summary grades to two decimal places—87.45 percent—in an effort to convince parents of their accuracy!

We should acknowledge measurement error, while at the same time, engaging in such practices as designing common assessments and moderated grading to increase the reliability of our assessments and, ultimately, of the grades we assign. Despite our best efforts, the processes of assessment and grading are, by nature, flawed. Consequently, the questioning of grades by students and parents is natural and understandable, and may necessitate having another professional review an assigned grade based on the evidence submitted.

8. The symbols used for grading purposes—percentages, letter grades, levels, and so on—must be accompanied by a set of appropriate indicators that are used consistently for all students. While teachers may need to exercise their professional judgment when assigning a grade to a student, depending on the individual circumstances, the *meaning* of that grade must be consistent for all students. An A assigned to a perennially high-achieving student

must mean the same as an A assigned to a student who has a history of struggling with learning. Hence, high grades must *not* be awarded to students on the basis of effort if the achievement is not worthy of an A. Students know when they have not met achievement standards and are simply being rewarded for trying hard.

9. Teachers must gather and summarize data about students' knowledge and skills separately from data about behaviors and attitudes. While both kinds of data are critical to learning, and may be highly correlated, they must be recorded and communicated separately to students and parents to ensure transparency and to facilitate improvement. See figure 9.6 for an example from a Canadian province-wide report card.

10. While poor grades have the potential to discourage further learning, grades should never be distorted in ways that deceive students and parents about the quality or amount of learning that has occurred. For struggling learners, the most common distortion occurs when effort is rewarded as a substitute for achievement. When a student works hard and does his or her best, that student deserves to be recognized for his or her effort. However, if the student is unable to meet a desired learning target, this information must be communicated clearly to the student and the parent.

Conclusion

If the mission of schools has changed from sifting and sorting students into high, average, and low achievers, it follows that the purpose of grading as well as the nature of grades must also change. Traditional grading practice—norm-referencing—has relied upon comparisons between students as the reference point for assigning grades. In norm-referenced systems, performance standards may change, depending on the achievement of the reference group. Hence, the practice of bell-curving results is common in such systems. That is, when too many students reach the desired standard, the standard is raised, despite the assessment having been completed. But when the new mission of schools is to bring *all* students to high levels of achievement on essential learning, grading must be referenced to clear, public standards of performance—criterion-referencing. And when increasing numbers of students meet these standards, the response must be celebration, not changing the standards!

Percentage Mark	
80–100	The student has demonstrated the required knowledge and skills with a high degree of effectiveness. Achievement surpasses the provincial standard. (Level 4)
70–79	The student has demonstrated the required knowledge and skills with considerable effectiveness. Achievement meets the provincial standard. (Level 3)
60–69	The student has demonstrated the required knowledge and skills with some effectiveness. Achievement approaches the provincial standard. (Level 2)
50–59	The student has demonstrated the required knowledge and skills with limited effectiveness. Achievement falls much below the provincial standard. (Level 1)
Below 50	The student has not demonstrated the required knowledge and skills. Extensive remediation is required.

Learning Skills and Work Habits E=Excellent G=Good S=Satisfactory N=Needs improvement	
Responsibility	**Organization**
• Fulfills responsibilities and commitments within the learning environment. • Completes and submits class work, homework, and assignments according to agreed upon timelines. • Takes responsibility for and manages own behavior.	• Devises and follows a plan and process for completing work and tasks. • Establishes priorities and manages time to complete tasks and achieve goals. • Identifies, gathers, evaluates, and uses information, technology, and resources to complete tasks.
Independent Work	**Collaboration**
• Independently monitors, assesses, and revises plans to complete tasks and meet goals. • Uses class time appropriately to complete tasks. • Follows instruction with minimal supervision.	• Accepts various roles and an equitable share of work in a group. • Responds positively to the ideas, opinions, values, and traditions of others. • Builds healthy, peer-to-peer relationships through personal and media-assisted interactions. • Works with others to resolve conflicts and build consensus to achieve group goals. • Shares information, resources, and expertise, and promotes critical thinking to solve problems and make decisions.
Initiative	**Self-Regulation**
• Looks for and acts on new ideas and opportunities for learning. • Demonstrates the capacity for innovation and a willingness to take risks. • Demonstrates curiosity and interest in learning. • Approaches new tasks with a positive attitude. • Recognizes and advocates appropriately for the rights of self and others.	• Sets own individual goals and monitors progress toward achieving them. • Seeks clarification or assistance when needed. • Assesses and reflects critically on own strengths, needs, and interests. • Identifies learning opportunities, choices, and strategies to meet personal needs and achieve goals. • Perseveres and makes an effort when responding to challenges.

© *Queen's Printer for Ontario, 2010. Reproduced with permission.*

Figure 9.6: Learning skills and work habits separated from achievement on a report card.

Because criterion-referenced grading relies upon clear, public performance standards, teachers must constantly examine and improve upon their practice to ensure that the grades they assign are meaningful, consistent, accurate, and supportive of learning. These are stringent criteria, and only through collaborative practices such as designing common assessments, moderated marking, and ongoing discussion can teachers ensure students and parents that the grades they assign meet them.

Teachers' understanding of grading must also include clarity about what grades represent. Does a grade provide information about growth, progress, or achievement? Measuring growth is necessary when working with young and struggling learners because such measures reflect improvement from baseline data and do not focus on how short of a standard a learner falls. Grading progress involves informing students and their parents how much progress has been made toward a prescribed standard, as measured from the previous reporting period. An achievement grade represents performance at a moment in time, regardless of whether growth or progress has occurred. Teachers need to understand these terms and use them intentionally when speaking with parents in order to avoid confusion about both the nature and the amount of learning that has occurred within a given term or semester.

While these definitions may imply that grading is a precise, theoretical process, it is not. Grading involves summarizing the learning that has occurred during a reporting period by assigning a rather crude symbol—a one-word descriptor, a score, a letter grade, or a level—to a sample of the work a student has produced. The very nature of this process demands that teachers bring to bear their professional judgment when assigning summary grades. Grades that support learning blend consistency with teachers' professional judgment. But professional judgment does *not* mean subjectivity! Subjectivity in grading occurs when teachers use their own, often idiosyncratic, criteria and procedures to determine summary grades. Professional judgment refers to decisions made by teachers in light of their experience and with reference to clear, public standards. To improve the quality and reliability of their professional judgments, teachers need to collaborate frequently in discussions about the meaning of the grades they assign, as well as the procedures they use to determine them. Finally, because grading student learning is at best a flawed process, teachers and administrators need to acknowledge the presence of measurement error and have in place clear and consistent procedures by which students and parents may question assessment data and summary grades.

CHAPTER 10

How Can I Report Effectively to Students in the Mixed-Ability Class and to Their Parents?

As I look at report card formats across Canada, the United States, and around the world, I am struck by how little attention is paid to the concepts of purpose and audience. The purpose of a report card is to provide students and parents with a brief summary of learning that has occurred during an instructional period. It should be seen as an invitation to deeper, more helpful communication with parents, and possibly with the student, to examine what has been learned, how well it has been learned, what remains to be learned, and the possible ways that parents may assist in further learning. The audience for the report card comprises, for the most part, noneducators who have little knowledge of curriculum, and who may or may not even be fluent in the first language of the school.

If all report cards were designed with purpose and audience in mind, I suspect the result would be dramatically different documents from those currently in circulation.

What Are Parents Looking For?

Let's consider what parents are looking for when they receive a report card from their child's school. They have a number of questions:

1. What has my child learned?

2. How well has my child demonstrated his or her learning?

3. What has my child not learned?

4. How can I help with what has not been learned?

5. How well behaved is my child?

What Has My Child Learned?

This is a curriculum question, of course, but we must remember that curriculum is written for teachers, not parents. Therefore, copying and pasting lengthy, convoluted standards or learning outcomes from curriculum documents into reporting templates is *not* appropriate! Furthermore, given limitations of space, report cards should identify essential learning, not specific facts or minor skills. Here is an appropriate example that identifies essential learning outcomes, in parent-friendly language, for two subject areas in grades 4–6 (fig. 10.1).

French	Social Studies
Uses familiar vocabulary to read and respond to a variety of texts	Demonstrates knowledge and understanding of concepts
Communicates written ideas using appropriate sentence structure	Uses a variety of resources and tools to research and record information
Speaks French in structured situations	Applies analytical and critical thinking
Speaks French in spontaneous situations	Communicates ideas and information using a variety of presentation tools
Listens in order to understand and respond appropriately for a variety of purposes	

Source: Interim Report Card (2006). Montcrest School, Toronto, Ontario. Used with permission.

Figure 10.1: Essential learning outcomes in parent-friendly language.

How Well Has My Child Demonstrated His or Her Learning?

This is the grading question and harkens back to the discussion in chapter 9 (page 123) about what the grades we assign really mean. Is a given grade a measure of achievement, progress, or growth? Furthermore, parents want to know, "Is my child doing as well as he or she should be?" Actually, most parents, based on their own experience, are really asking, "How well is my child doing compared to his or her peers?" However, today's report cards more typically reflect criterion-referenced data. It follows that if parents are to understand the meaning of the grades their child has received, the frame of reference must appear on the report card. Figure 10.2 provides an example.

This section indicates how your child is performing in relation to the course and grade-level outcomes in the Alberta Program of Studies.

Reporting Key			
Beginning:	**Developing:**	**Achieving:**	**Extending:**
Your child needs more time and support in developing the learner outcomes. Students at the Beginning level are not yet meeting grade level performance standards expected at this point of the school year and need additional instructional opportunities to meet grade level standards.	Your child demonstrates basic academic performance which indicates a partial understanding of the learner outcomes. Students at the Developing level of performance are meeting the minimum grade level performance standards expected at this point of the school year.	Your child demonstrates consistent academic performance which indicates a solid understanding of the learner outcomes. Students at the Achieving level of performance are meeting the accepted grade level performance standards expected at this point of the school year.	Your child demonstrates exemplary academic performance by extending their learning and applying their knowledge in a variety of situations. Students at the Extending level of performance have an in-depth understanding of grade level performance standards expected at this point of the school year.

Not Addressed:		**Not Applicable:**	**Incomplete:**
This concept or skill has not been addressed during this reporting period and will be addressed later in the year.		This learner outcome is not included in the Program of Studies at this particular grade level.	There is insufficient evidence of learning to accurately assess progress of learner outcomes during this reporting period.

Source: Learner Profile 2009–2010 (p. 2). Foothills School Division, Alberta, Canada. Used with permission.

Figure 10.2: Academic achievement.

Looking at a student's achievement in language arts for the first term, a parent in this school division might receive the summary in figure 10.3 (page 144).

Language Arts	Reporting Period	Reporting Period	Reporting Period
Teacher:	1	2	3
Reading	Achieving		
Writing	Achieving		
Speaking	Beginning		
Listening	Developing		
Viewing	Achieving		
Representing	Achieving		

Source: Learner Profile 2009–2010 (p. 2). Foothills School Division, Alberta, Canada. Used with permission.

Figure 10.3: Summary of student achievement in language arts.

What Has My Child Not Learned?

Again, this is a curriculum question, but it is a more difficult one to answer because it concerns gaps and deficits rather than achievements. While the sample above indicates that this student is struggling with the oral component of language arts, the parent requires more detailed information about precisely what kinds of difficulties the child is having and how these difficulties might be addressed. While an appropriate anecdotal comment, such as the one that follows, can help in this regard, email, telephone, or (ideally) face-to-face communication will be necessary to discuss next steps—a plan of action to improve this student's oral skills.

> Students are expected to share orally their responses to books and videos, as well as to listen and comment on the views of others. However, Brad needs to improve both his speaking and listening skills. He is encouraged to practice these skills at home.

How Can I Help With What Has Not Been Learned?

Many school districts direct teachers to compose anecdotal report card comments using a consistent three-part formula:

1. Identify areas of strength.

2. Identify areas of need.

3. Indicate suggestions for improvement, including parental support.

In Brad's case, a more complete language arts comment might read as follows:

> Brad willingly reads a variety of texts, using appropriate strategies to aid his comprehension. He uses the writing process effectively to move from first drafts to polished work. Brad demonstrates strong receptive communication skills when viewing instructional videos and representing his learning using various media. However, Brad needs to improve both his speaking and listening skills. Students are expected to share orally their responses to books and videos, as well as to listen and comment on the views of others. He is encouraged to practice these skills at home.

The last sentence begs the question, what might we do as parents to assist in this practice? Because both time and space constraints typically limit the amount of detail contained in reporting comments, this question is best addressed through a phone call or email between the parent and teacher. Such informal communication may reveal that Brad is in the habit of rushing dinner and then running off to his room. His teacher might suggest to his parents that meal times could provide regular opportunities for Brad to practice his speaking and listening skills.

How Well Behaved Is My Child?

As we saw in chapter 9 (page 123), and as illustrated in figure 10.4 (page 146), effective report cards distinguish clearly between data relating to student achievement and information about attitudes and behaviors.

Academic Skills			
Language	Grade	**Mathematics**	Grade
Reads and understands information from a variety of sources, using a range of strategies to construct meaning		Demonstrates an understanding of concepts	
Generates, plans and organizes ideas and information for written work		Applies mathematical procedures accurately	
Uses a variety of editing strategies to refine written work		Performs mathematical computations accurately	
Proofreads to correct mechanics and spelling in written work		Uses precise mathematical language to communicate understanding	
Listens in order to understand and respond appropriately for a variety of purposes (e.g., summarize, make notes)		Solves mathematical problems accurately by selecting appropriate strategies	
Speaks with clarity and precision to communicate for a variety of purposes (e.g., ask, explain, comment)		**History and Geography**	
French		Demonstrates knowledge and understanding of concepts	
Uses familiar vocabulary to read and respond to a variety of texts		Uses a variety of resources and tools to research and record information	
Communicates written ideas using appropriate sentence structure		Thinks analytically and critically, to communicate from more than one point of view	
Speaks French in structured situations		Communicates ideas and information using a variety of presentation tools	
Speaks French in spontaneous situations			

Learning Skills			
Respect Responsibility Integrity Compassion Courage			
E – With extensive support F – With frequent support S – With some support I - Independently			
	Grade		Grade
Demonstrates **respect** for others, property, and the code of conduct		Shows **integrity** through honesty and self-discipline	
Takes academic **responsibility** by asking questions and self-advocating		Demonstrates **compassion** for others through words and actions	
Takes personal **responsibility** for managing materials, time, and tasks		Shows **courage** by taking risks and showing initiative	
Homeroom Comment:			

Source: Interim Report Card (2006). Montcrest School, Toronto, Ontario. Used with permission.

Figure 10.4: Report card that distinguishes achievement from behavior and attitude.

Report cards that separate information about achievement in knowledge and skills from information about attitudes and behaviors provide parents with clear, useful data that they can use to support their children's improvement. For older students, separate summaries from these two domains also enable postsecondary institutions, as well as part-time and full-time employers, to fully understand the strengths and areas of need exhibited by students applying for further education or employment. Figure 10.5 shows Roberto's report card with his letter grades.

Academic Skills			
Science	Grade	**Music**	Grade
Demonstrates knowledge and understanding of concepts	B	**Art**	
Communicates the procedures and results of investigations	D	**Drama**	
Analyzes and synthesizes information to draw conclusions	D	**Physical Education**	
Homeroom Comment:			
Learning Skills			
Respect Responsibility Integrity Compassion Courage			
E – With extensive support F – With frequent support S – With some support I - Independently			
	Grade		Grade
Demonstrates **respect** for others, property, and the code of conduct	S	Shows **integrity** through honesty and self-discipline	
Takes academic **responsibility** by asking questions and self-advocating	E	Demonstrates **compassion** for others through words and actions	
Takes personal **responsibility** for managing materials, time, and tasks	E	Shows **courage** by taking risks and showing initiative	
Homeroom Comment: *You can see from Roberto's report card . . .*			

Figure 10.5: Roberto's report card with letter grades.

Report cards such as the one shown in figure 10.5 enable parents to see the relationship between achievement data and their child's learning skills and behaviors. A comment can then serve to further explain this relationship:

> You can see from Roberto's report card that he has a D in two of the science outcomes. You can also see that he requires

extensive support in both "responsibility" areas. This is because he has not yet acquired the science skills he needs to conduct his own inquiries, analyze his findings, and communicate them. He is falling behind because he is reluctant to try these skills for himself. Instead, he prefers to ask me before attempting things himself. We need to work together to help Roberto develop the confidence to work independently.

Such comments pave the way for the teacher and parents to collaborate on ways to increase Roberto's confidence.

Clarity About the Meaning of Grades on Report Cards

If the reporting format used at your school uses descriptors that contain the words *progress* and *progressing*, then it must be clear to parents which targets students are progressing toward, because progress is a measure of how close the student is to a desired end point. The sample illustrated in figure 10.6 does *not* meet this criterion because there is no set of indicators to interpret the three degrees of progress.

A principal at a workshop told me that the ambiguity of terms such as *progressing with difficulty, progressing well,* and *progressing very well* was causing significant communication problems between the teachers in her school and parents when they met following a midterm reporting period. Clear, effective communication with parents demands that growth, progress, and achievement terms be referenced to scales that appear on report cards. Without such scales, teachers will continue to complain that reporting is subjective, and parents will continue to be denied the detailed and specific information they need to understand their child's current levels of skill and understanding and what they need to do to improve.

Appropriate reporting formats for kindergarten and the early primary grades employ descriptors that refer to *growth,* rather than progress or achievement. Hence, they use terms such as *beginning, developing,* and *secure,* as illustrated in figure 10.7 (page 150). Part of the report card may be found in reproducible form on page 173. Visit **go.solution-tree.com/instruction** to download it in its entirety. Note that while this report card has many excellent features, it also fails to provide parents with a set of indicators to explain the three levels of growth.

Elementary Progress Report Card				
Student				**Grade**
ESL/ELD—Achievement is based on expectations modified from the curriculum expectations for the grade to support English language learning needs. **IEP—**Individual Education Plan **NA—**No instruction for subject/strand				**Strengths/Next Steps for Improvement**
Subjects	Progressing With Difficulty	Progressing Well	Progressing Very Well	
Language				
Reading, Writing, Oral Communication, Media Literacy ☐ ESL/ELD ☐ IEP ☐ NA				
French				
☐ ESL/ELD ☐ IEP ☐ NA ☐ Core ☐ Immersion ☐ Extended				
Native Language				
☐ ESL/ELD ☐ IEP ☐ NA				
Mathematics				
☐ ESL/ELD ☐ IEP ☐ French				
Science and Technology				
☐ ESL/ELD ☐ IEP ☐ French				
Social Studies				
☐ ESL/ELD ☐ IEP ☐ French				
Health Education				
☐ ESL/ELD ☐ IEP ☐ French				
Physical Education				
☐ ESL/ELD ☐ IEP ☐ French				

Figure 10.6: Report format lacking progress indicators.

B = Beginning D = Developing S = Secure			The expectations for achievement are that students will meet Secure (S) proficiency levels by spring. The shaded area indicates when the outcome is usually first assessed.

Writing Genre

F	W	S	Concepts/Skills
▓			1. Writes a brief personal story using pictures, words, and/or sentences.
		▓	2. Reads and tries to copy different styles of poetry.
		▓	3. Writes a brief informational piece using drawings, words, and/or sentences as a page for a class book.
		▓	4. Helps with a class research project by adding key information gathered from materials supplied by the teacher.

Writing Process

F	W	S	
▓			5. Brainstorms ideas for narrative stories.
▓			6. Produces pictures and drawings that fit the story.
	▓		7. As s/he plans to write, with help from the teacher, thinks about how the readers will react.
	▓		8. Spells words based on how they sound when writing.
		▓	9. Brainstorms ideas for informational text.
		▓	10. Makes changes to writing by reading it to a friend, and asks for ideas to improve it to make the meaning more clear.

Personal Style

F	W	S	
	▓		11. Expresses feelings, uses his/her natural language, and creates new ideas to show originality in his/her speech and writing.

Spelling

F	W	S	
	▓		12. Uses beginning and simple ending sounds, or word lists provided by the teacher to figure out how to spell more words.
		▓	13. Correctly spells about 18 words s/he sees often and finds meaningful.

Handwriting

F	W	S	
▓			14. Writes from left to right and top to bottom.
	▓		15. Forms upper- and lowercase letters.
		▓	16. Leaves spaces between words when writing.

Writing Attitude

F	W	S	
▓	▓	▓	17. Is eager to write and learn to write.

Source: Kindergarten Report, 2009 (p. 1). Ann Arbor Public Schools, Ann Arbor, MI. Used with permission.

Figure 10.7: Reporting format with growth descriptors.

To provide meaningful, useful information to parents, schools should ensure that growth-oriented report cards are aligned with corresponding developmental continua such as the one shown again in figure 10.8.

Visit **go.solution-tree.com/instruction** to download the full continuum.

Developmental Aspects	Emerging With Direct Support . . .	Developing With Guided Support . . .	Applying With Minimal Support . . .	Extending
	→	→	→	→
The Child	With direct support may draw on personal connections while participating in a variety of reading/viewing experiences to make meaning.	With guided support draws on and begins to develop strategies (e.g., making connections, predicting, asking questions, and reflecting) while participating in a variety of reading/viewing experiences to make meaning.	With minimal support draws on and expands strategies (e.g., making connections, predicting, asking questions, and reflecting) while participating in a variety of reading/viewing experiences to make meaning.	Draws on, expands, and begins to identify strategies (e.g., making connections, predicting, asking questions, and reflecting) while participating in a variety of reading/viewing experiences to make meaning.
Thinking/Metacognition				
Developing dispositions— awareness, attention, interest, participation, curiosity, engagement, perseverance	With direct support may attend to and may participate in reading/viewing activities (e.g., makes meaning from text using pictures, pattern, memory, prior knowledge).	With guided support engages in reading/ viewing activities (e.g., makes meaning from text using pictures, pattern, memory, prior knowledge).	With minimal support purposefully engages in reading/viewing activities (e.g., makes meaning from text using pictures, pattern, memory, prior knowledge).	Purposefully engages in reading/viewing activities (e.g., makes meaning from text using emergent reading strategies).
Setting purpose	With direct support may participate in setting purpose for reading/ viewing.	With guided support sets a purpose for reading/viewing.	With minimal support chooses a purpose for reading/viewing.	Identifies a purpose for reading/viewing; participates in the reading/viewing process.

*A variety of supports (teachers, peers, environmental, etc.) can be provided at any stage of development.

Source: Kindergarten Learning Project (2008). Grateful acknowledgment to the Kindergarten Learning Project Team, the British Columbia Ministry of Education, and Qualicum British Columbia School District 69. Reprinted with permission.

Figure 10.8: Continuum to accompany a growth-oriented report card.

Clearly, a detailed continuum such as this would not appear on the report card itself but would be included as an attachment. The continuum also provides the focus for face-to-face discussions with parents after a report card has been sent home. Visit **go.solution-tree.com/instruction** to download kindergarten developmental continua for both reading/viewing and writing/ representing.

Finally, if a report card is to communicate information about proficiency or achievement, then it must be aligned with a set of performance standards—preferably criterion-referenced—which enable students and parents to interpret current proficiency/achievement levels relative to those standards. In the example in figure 10.9, a school district explains to parents how the numerical grades should be interpreted with respect to the end of the school year:

WHAT CAN YOU EXPECT TO SEE ON THE STANDARDS-BASED REPORT CARDS?

Based on the child's performance, one of the following scores will be given:

- A score of 1 indicates below end-of-the-year grade-level standards.
- A score of 2 indicates approaching end-of-the-year grade-level standards.
- A score of 3 indicates at end-of-the-year grade-level standards.
- A score of 4 indicates advanced end-of-the-year grade-level standards.

It is not unusual for a child to receive several 2s on the first and second trimester report card, because a score of 3 indicates a mastery level that is usually attained toward the end of the school year.

Source: Academic Standards Trimester Report (2007). Murrieta Valley Unified School District, Murrieta, California. Used with permission.

Figure 10.9. Explanation to parents of how to interpret numerical grades.

The full, corresponding report card (available at **go.solution-tree.com /instruction**) contains the following outstanding features:

- A reasonable number of standards for each subject area, providing parents and students with sufficient information about areas of strength and need
- Standards that are phrased in user-friendly language
- A four-level achievement scale clarifying for parents that the standards represent end-of-year targets. They should not expect their child to be achieving at levels 3 or 4 before the third trimester!

Can Grades Communicate Both Progress and Achievement?

Let's return to the comment posed by the teacher at the beginning of chapter 9 (page 123)—that her students work really hard and make progress but still only manage to get Cs and Ds.

Is it possible to design a report card that communicates information to students and their parents about achievement *and* progress? I believe it is, as do Wiggins (1994b) and Wormeli (2006). Such reporting does require some additional recordkeeping by teachers; it also assumes that parents are willing to accept more complex data about their children. Consider the report card excerpt in figure 10.10.

Name: Joshua Smith	**Grade:** 6	
Achievement Scale		
A- to A+	Student demonstrates solid control of, or mastery of required skills.	
B- to B+	Student demonstrates good to very good control of required skills.	
C- to C+	Student demonstrates inconsistent control of required skills.	
D- to D+	Student demonstrates very limited to limited control of required skills.	

Progress Scale

The numbers indicate the number of levels a student has progressed since the beginning of the term. There are 12 levels: D-, D, D+, C-, C, C+, B-, B, B+, A-, A, A+

A progress level of 2 means the student has progressed by 2 levels. A progress level of 0 means the student has not progressed.

Language Arts

	Achievement	Progress
Reading	C-	2
Writing	C	2
Oral Communication	B-	1
Media Literacy	B	2

Comment:

As shown, Joshua has made steady progress in three of the strands. While he has shown some progress in oral communication, he continues to be very quiet during our literature circles. He would benefit from frequent opportunities to respond orally to events, the media, and other topics at home.

Figure 10.10: Term 1 report card showing both achievement and progress.

Joshua's achievement grades on each of the strands of the language program are C-, C, B-, and B.

The numbers 2, 2, 1, and 2 indicate Joshua's progress with respect to each of the language strands during an instructional period. These are measures of the number of levels he has progressed in each strand, starting from initial diagnostic assessment data and measured up to the first reporting period.

On the second-term report card, these numbers would represent the number of levels he has progressed since the first reporting period.

With the addition of this progress data, Joshua's parents gain a much deeper understanding of the trend in their son's learning and achievement. For Joshua, while there is still plenty of room for improvement, he can feel pride and a sense of accomplishment about the progress he is making.

Reporting for Students With Special Needs

Clearly, reporting progress as well as achievement is vital for struggling students. During a recent workshop, an elementary teacher asked me, "Damian, how do I explain to the parents of a special needs student with an IEP that the A she has received is for a modified program and that it doesn't mean the same as the As received by other children in the class who are working at grade level?"

This question reflects a number of extremely important yet often misunderstood principles of instruction and assessment. As I have explained throughout this book, the goal of teaching should be to have all students demonstrate proficiency on essential skills and understanding at grade level, and to do so independently. When initial or formative assessments indicate that a student is unable to do this, the teacher begins to differentiate the program. This process begins with the teacher making accommodations to instruction or assessment conditions. These may include changes to materials, instructional strategies, environmental conditions, or a combination of these. Typically, report cards do not require that such accommodations be communicated to parents.

If, on the other hand, the student is unable to demonstrate success despite accommodations being in place, the teacher may need to modify part of the student's program. I say *part*, because in language arts, for example, the student may need modifications in reading but not in writing or in speaking. Modification usually involves having the student work on learning targets from a lower grade level. Most jurisdictions require that modifications be noted on the report card with statements such as "This grade reflects achievement of learning outcomes at _____ grade level," in which the level entered in the space differs from the grade in which the child is currently registered.

Now comes the challenging and most often misunderstood part of the scenario. It is not appropriate that the child in question achieve a grade of A on his or her report card if he or she is receiving a modified program. Why? Because if the student is able to achieve an A, he or she should not receive a modified program! To explain, if Alex is registered in grade 5 but her teacher has determined that she is unable to experience success in reading, even with accommodations in place, the decision is made to modify her program such that she will work on grade 3 learning outcomes. This means she will read texts at the grade 3 level and complete other assessment tasks related to reading that are at the grade 3 level. At the first reporting period, Alex receives a C for reading, with the notation that this represents achievement on learning outcomes that are two grade levels below the expectations for her class. Figure 10.11 provides descriptors that are used to define the letter grades used at Alex's school.

A	Proficient
B	Competent
C	Satisfactory
D	Unsatisfactory
R	Significant remediation necessary

Figure 10.11: Descriptors for letter grades.

As the second term progresses, Alex's reading skills improve dramatically. At this point, her teacher begins to present Alex with reading materials that are at the grade 4 level—remember, the goal is to have Alex demonstrate proficiency at grade level. On the second-term report card, Alex receives a C grade, and the teacher writes the following comment:

> Alex has demonstrated significant improvement in reading and is now demonstrating satisfactory achievement on texts that are at the grade 4 level. With continued hard work, I expect that Alex will be working at grade level by the final term. Congratulations, Alex!

It would be inappropriate teaching and reporting practice to have Alex continue experiencing a modified program in reading—working on below-grade-level learning outcomes—as her skills improve, and to assign a report card grade of A. Effective differentiation requires the teacher to constantly monitor a student's levels of skill and understanding and to continually adjust the zone of proximal development (chapter 5, page 73) to ensure that the student is challenged but not frustrated by the work she is expected to do. Hence, as soon as the student demonstrates reading skills at the satisfactory level on below-grade outcomes, the teacher needs to introduce reading materials aligned with the next grade level.

Conclusion

Many of the problems reflected in current reporting formats occur because the designers did not begin with a clear sense of purpose and audience. Simply asking who reads the report card and what purposes it must achieve would lead to improvements in four areas:

1. **Brevity**—Two pages seem to be the optimum length. The report card is an invitation to in-depth follow-up communication during student/parent/teacher interviews.

2. **Clarity**—The symbols used to grade learning as well as their associated descriptors must be clear and include minimal education jargon. Information about understanding and skills must be reported separately from information about behaviors and attitudes. Anecdotal comments must provide explanations about these two areas, as well as useful suggestions for parents to support the learner.

3. **Transparency**—All information must be truthful, recognizing that sensitive issues will be dealt with during face-to-face follow-up communication.

4. **Responsiveness**—There should be a place for the student or parent to comment upon the contents of the report card.

As school systems around the world move away from norm-referenced grading and increasingly embrace criterion-referenced grading, parents, communities, and postsecondary institutions need to be educated about the changing nature of reporting on learning. Outside of the K–12 educational community, there continues to be the expectation that rigorous grading and reporting ranks students, one against another, in a winners and losers race to the finish line. Through our formal and informal reporting methods, schools need to educate all stakeholders so that they understand that effective summaries of student learning *describe* and *rate* learning, according to public performance standards. Such education is a complex task that will take time. But an important first step is for schools to communicate how grading and reporting practices and procedures are changing through brief, simply worded explanations on school websites, in attachments to the report card, and during parent information sessions.

EPILOGUE

As educators, we are in the midst of unprecedented change. Curriculum is changing as developers wrestle with the question: what should we be teaching students in the 21st century? Our instructional repertoire is expanding as we learn more about how children learn and as technology pervades everything we do. The role of assessment is evolving as we discover its potential to not merely measure learning, but to improve it. Grading practices are being scrutinized as the mission of schools shifts from sifting and sorting students into winners and losers to ensuring that *all* students develop understanding and proficiency with respect to essential learning targets. And most importantly, our students are changing in terms of where they come from, how they learn, and what they need from their teachers if they are to become fulfilled, productive citizens of the global village.

For all of these reasons, we must, as professionals, continue to improve our craft. This means we must constantly reflect upon our current practices. Working collegially, we must examine what is working and what is not—and problem solve to become more effective teachers.

Every classroom today needs to be differentiated. This book has sought to provide you with strategies that make differentiation effective and manageable. *Effective* means that opportunities to learn are optimized for *all* students; *manageable* means that you do not lose your mind while doing this! Most teachers tell me they have not received sufficient training, either during preservice or through professional development programs, to be able to plan, teach, assess, and grade effectively in mixed-ability classes. This book is a response to your pleas for help. But your colleagues are your best professional learning resource. The case studies and strategies that I have written about come from your peers, not from me! There are colleagues in your school and in your district who are already skilled in planning for a variety of student needs: colleagues who already employ a broad repertoire of effective instructional strategies, recognizing the many ways by which children learn; colleagues who understand how to assess in ways that are responsive to individual differences. Seek them out and work with them. Arrange to collaborate on the design of a unit; plan a common assessment and engage in a moderated marking session in which you examine students' work and refine your performance standards; lobby your colleagues and collectively suggest to your principal that your school's PLC (professional learning community) focus for next year be differentiation strategies. Each of these initiatives demands that you take control of your own professional development.

The quest for excellence is a theme in this book, but as I have suggested, there exist many ill-conceived notions about what constitutes excellence! A commitment to excellence begins when we believe deeply that every child has the potential to excel in something. When we truly believe that every child has the capacity to succeed, we no longer speak about A students. Because if there are A students, then there are also F students! Such language suggests that we are mere child-minders, *not* teachers; that students come into our classes as A, B, C, or D students; and that our job is to see that they leave that way.

There are no A *students;* there are only A *performances.* It is our responsibility as teachers to create the conditions in which every child can imagine himself or herself excelling. Teaching high achievers is easy. But when struggling students say they don't care about excellence, we have to push them and demand that they produce quality work. We excel as teachers when those struggling students experience the joy of success and feel pride in their work for the first time. For us, *that* is quality work.

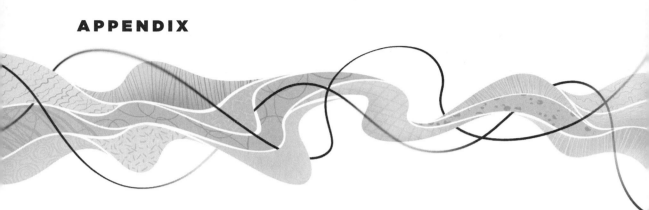

Reproducibles

Differentiated Instruction Continuum

Use this self-identification tool to determine your level of readiness with respect to the classroom application of differentiated instruction.

PREIMPLEMENTATION — Developing Instructional Routines and Skills	IMPLEMENTATION — Expanding Instructional Routines and Skills	BUILDING CAPACITY — Developing the Routines, Habits, and Skills for Differentiated Instruction	SUSTAINING CAPACITY — Sustaining a Differentiated Instruction Culture in the Classroom
Modeling to Learners	Shared Practice With Learners	Guided Practice With Learners	Independent Practice by Learners
I design instruction, assessment, evaluation, and the learning environment for the class as a whole based on curriculum expectations and my own strengths and preferences.	I design instruction, assessment, evaluation, and the learning environment based on curriculum expectations and a general sense of the learning needs of the class.	I design instruction, assessment, evaluation, and the learning environment based on curriculum expectations and a general sense of the learning needs of the class. I try to design a variety of options for my students.	I design instruction, assessment, evaluation, and the learning environment based on curriculum expectations and on the specific learning needs of the students in the class. I try to ensure that the learning experiences I provide are a "good fit" for each of my students.
I model while students observe and try to understand.	I work together with students. I model and help students complete the activities.	Students complete the activities while I help them.	Students work independently by adopting my model while I observe.
All students learn and demonstrate their learning in the same way all or most of the time.	Students experience, over time, a variety of ways to learn and/or ways to demonstrate their learning.	Students have a choice of ways to learn and/or ways to demonstrate their learning on an ongoing basis.	Students are routinely provided with, or choose when appropriate, ways to learn and/or ways to demonstrate their learning that are designed for their particular learning needs.
Examples: Anticipation guide, exit card, graphic organizers, supplementary materials	**Examples:** Activities for all that address different learning styles or intelligences on different days, multiple entry points for all / Over time, varied supplementary materials	**Examples:** Differentiation structures that offer choice: centers, Choice Boards, RAFT* assignments / Choice of supplementary materials	**Examples:** Differentiation structures such as RAFT* and tiered assignments / Provision of, or as appropriate, student choice of supplementary materials based on their needs
Same for all students		Different options for different students	
LITTLE DIFFERENTIATION		MUCH DIFFERENTIATION	

*RAFT = role, audience, format, topic

© *Queen's Printer for Ontario, 2007. Reproduced with permission.*

Grade 8 Language Arts Lesson
Differentiation Details

Making Inferences While Listening (Oral Communication 1.5) & Metacognition (Oral Communication 3.1)

Text: "Sibling Secrets," in K. Hume & B. Ledgerwood, *Nelson literacy 8* (pp. 35–37). Toronto, ON: Nelson Education.

Ability Groupings

Character Groupings: Salims (Level 2s), Abidas (Level 3s), & Ghazalas (Level 4s). Groupings based on students' pre-assessment data for inferencing (DRA Data)

Three-Member Groups: One student from each level; thus, level 4 students can model reading skills to level 2 & 3 students

Differentiated Learning Supports

Small Group Sessions: Sessions take place each class where students are invited to work with myself at the round table. Students selected are rotated between the different levels. This is to serve as a support system where students can brainstorm with students of the same ability.

Conference Group Sessions: Sessions take place each class, with students invited to work at the back conference station. Students selected are rotated between the different levels. This is to serve as a support system where students can brainstorm with students of the same ability.

SMART Board Station: Students are invited to write their responses on the SMART Board. Allows for a hands-on experience for the learner.

Teacher for the Period: One student is selected at the beginning of each period to be the go-to-person for questions and concerns about the task at hand. They get to sit at the teacher's desk. If they are unsure of an answer, they can ask me. This strategy allows me to have more available time for small group sessions and informal conferencing while also placing the student in the spotlight!

Source: Personal communication, Holly Miskelly, January 18, 2010. Used with permission.

Classroom Design:	• Around the room, the students have various supports to their learning. The 'work exemplar' station at the back has point/proof explanation examples from the shared strategy of making inferences. Students are welcome to visit these examples while working on their task to support them.
	• The organizer of the week section in the Learning Support Station has various graphic organizers from the unit to help assist the learner while working.
	• Class materials are at the front along with a basket. Students may borrow any material that they are in need of by placing a personal item in the basket. This way, I am assured that I will receive my materials back and the students can focus on their work, as opposed to focusing on finding materials.
	• The Word Wall section is placed beside the small group section, so that the words are accessible while working with the students in a smaller session. Word Wall includes vocabulary from both the social studies unit and language units being studied.
	• Today's schedule is placed in the learning support station to remind the students who are unsure of the task at hand what is expected of them during the period.
Assessment of Learning:	Exit Pass reflecting on the students' understanding of one high-yield strategy to help them improve their inferencing skills.
Assessment for Learning:	Informal student/teacher "check-in" points throughout the work period time to ensure that students understand the components of the skills.
Evaluation:	Nelson Literacy 8b Series Rubric, Making Inferences While Listening, designed for "Sibling Secrets," in K. Hume & B. Ledgerwood, *Nelson Literacy 8* (pp. 35–37). Toronto, ON: Nelson Education.

Source: Personal communication, Holly Miskelly, January 18, 2010. Used with permission.

Grade 8 Language Arts Lesson
Differentiation Details

Making Inferences: Level 1–2 Graphic Organizer

Inference #1

Point: (State your inference.)

Proof: (Use text clues + prior knowledge to support answer.)

Explanation: (Relate your inference to the author's message.)

Inference #2

Point: (State your inference.)

Proof: (Use text clues + prior knowledge to support answer.)

Explanation: (Relate your inference to the author's message.)

Metacognition Question: How does using the point/proof/explanation model help you to create a stronger inference? Explain your answers.

_____

_____

_____

_____

Source: Personal communication, Holly Miskelly, January 18, 2010. Used with permission.

Grade 8 Language Arts Lesson
Differentiation Details

Making Inferences: Level 3 Graphic Organizer

Text Clues +	Prior Knowledge =	Inference
		Point: (State your inference.) **Proof:** (Use text clues and prior knowledge to support answer.) **Explanation:** (Relate your inference to the author's message.)

Metacognition Question: How does using the point/proof/explanation model help you to create a stronger inference? Explain your answers.

_____

_____

_____

_____

_____

Source: Personal communication, Holly Miskelly, January 18, 2010. Used with permission.

Grade 8 Language Arts Lesson
Differentiation Details

Making Inferences: Level 4 Graphic Organizer

Inference # 1

Guiding Inferencing Question: (Use Q chart to establish question.)

Inference Response:

Inference # 2

Guiding Inferencing Question: (Use Q chart to establish question.)

Inference Response:

Metacognition Question: How does creating your own guiding inferencing questions allow you to have a deeper understanding of the test? Explain.

_____

_____

_____

_____

_____

Source: Personal communication, Holly Miskelly, January 18, 2010. Used with permission.

Grade 8 Language Arts Lesson
Differentiation Details

Level 4 Support: The "Q" Chart

The Q chart below gives a framework for creating questions. Start your question with a word from the first column and add a verb from the top row. The combination you choose will drive your question.

	Is	Did	Can	Would	Will	Might
What						
Where			Level 1		Level 3	
When						
Who						
Why			Level 2		Level 4	
How						

Source: Personal communication, Holly Miskelly, January 18, 2010. Used with permission.

Grade 8 Language Arts Lesson Differentiation Details

Rubric: Making Inferences While Listening

Name: _____ Date: _____

- Identify and use a variety of comprehension strategies to clarify the meaning of oral texts.
- Develop/explain interpretations of oral texts by using oral/visual clues from the texts.

Criteria	Level 1	Level 2	Level 3	Level 4
Infers the speaker's perspective on the topic	Makes simple inferences about the speaker's perspective T1☐ T2☐ T3☐	Makes increasingly complex inferences about the speaker's perspective T1☐ T2☐ T3☐	Makes complex inferences about the speaker's perspective T1☐ T2☐ T3☐	Makes highly complex inferences about the speaker's perspective T1☐ T2☐ T3☐
Compares the speaker's perspective to personal perspectives on the topic	Makes simplistic comparisons T1☐ T2☐ T3☐	Makes increasingly relevant comparisons T1☐ T2☐ T3☐	Makes insightful comparisons T1☐ T2☐ T3☐	Makes complex comparisons T1☐ T2☐ T3☐
Notes new information	Notes a few pieces of information T1☐ T2☐ T3☐	Notes some new information T1☐ T2☐ T3☐	Notes most new information T1☐ T2☐ T3☐	Notes all/almost all new information T1☐ T2☐ T3☐
Uses the speaker's tone, mood, body language, and facial expressions to make inferences	Uses the speaker's tone, mood, body language, and facial expressions to infer simple implicit messages T1☐ T2☐ T3☐	Uses the speaker's tone, mood, body language, and facial expressions to infer increasingly complex implicit messages T1☐ T2☐ T3☐	Uses the speaker's tone, mood, body language, and facial expressions to infer complex implicit messages T1☐ T2☐ T3☐	Uses the speaker's tone, mood, body language, and facial expressions to infer highly complex implicit messages T1☐ T2☐ T3☐
Records important information while listening	Records a few pieces of important information T1☐ T2☐ T3☐	Records some important information T1☐ T2☐ T3☐	Records most important information T1☐ T2☐ T3☐	Records all/most all important information T1☐ T2☐ T3☐
• Explains how making inferences while listening helps the listener understand oral texts	• Demonstrates limited knowledge of how the strategy helps the listener T1☐ T2☐ T3☐	• Demonstrates some knowledge of how the strategy helps the listener T1☐ T2☐ T3☐	• Demonstrates considerable knowledge of how the strategy helps the listener T1☐ T2☐ T3☐	• Demonstrates thorough knowledge of how the strategy helps the listener T1☐ T2☐ T3☐
Cross-Curricular Application Applies the skills involved in making inferences while listening in other subject areas	Applies the skills, with limited effectiveness T4☐	Applies the skills, with some effectiveness T4☐	Applies the skills, with considerable effectiveness T4☐	Applies the skills, with a high degree of effectiveness T4☐

Source: Personal communication, Holly Miskelly, January 18, 2010. Used with permission.

Support Materials for Claudette Oegema's Grade 3 Language Arts Lesson

A.P.E. Checklist—Self

Did I use three highlighters?	Yes	No
Do I have three sentences?	Yes	No
Did I start each sentence with a capital?	Yes	No
Did I use my pink words in my first sentence?	Yes	No
Did I prove my point? (Did I mention baseball?)	Yes	No
Did I make a self to text connection? (Did I talk about playing or watching baseball?)	Yes	No

I like how I _____

_____

_____

_____

I need to work on _____

_____

_____

_____

A.P.E. Checklist—Peer

Did your partner use three highlighters?	Yes	No
Do he or she have three sentences?	Yes	No
Did he or she start each sentence with a capital?	Yes	No
Did he or she use their pink words in the first sentence?	Yes	No
Did your partner prove his or her point? (Did he or she mention baseball?)	Yes	No
Did your partner make a self to text connection? (Did he or she talk about playing or watching baseball?)	Yes	No

I like how I _____

_____

_____

_____

I need to work on _____

_____

_____

_____

Source: Personal communication, C. Oegema, January 29, 2009. Used with permission.

Materials to Support Grade 10 Mathematics Class

MFM2P Measurement Practice Test

Name: _____

By the end of the course, students will: use the imperial and metric systems of measurement.

Category	Questions	R	1	2	3	4
KU	1					
KU	2					
KU	3					
A	4					
A	5					
A	6					
C	best					

Part 1: Knowledge

Answer each question to the best of your ability. Show enough work so that I know what you're doing.

1. Convert each of the following. Show your calculations.

    a) 75 inches to centimeters   b) 13 kilograms to pounds

2. Carefully measure the triangle and calculate its perimeter and area. Show enough work so that I know what you're doing.

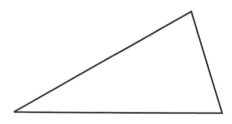

Source: Created by Julia Bilenkis. Adapted with permission.

3. The picture shows an outdoor thermometer.

   a) Are the numbers around the circumference of the thermometer in Celsius or Fahrenheit degrees? Explain how you know.

   b) Convert the temperature to the <u>other</u> unit.

Part 2: Application

Product Specifications Corr Grain Bin		
Weight	1958.1 kg	4300 lb.
Diameter	6.37 m	20' 10 ½"

4. Examine the product specifications above.

   a) The weight conversion is a bit off. Verify this and correct it.

   b) Check the diameter conversion. How good is it?

5. An ice hockey arena has

   • 22 km of steel refrigeration pipe for the rink

   • 17 miles of yellow lines in the parking lot

   • 11,900 feet of roof truss

Compare the three measurements. Which is the largest? Be sure to show your reasoning and calculations.

Source: Created by Julia Bilenkis. Adapted with permission.

Redefining Fair © 2011 Solution Tree Press · solution-tree.com
Visit **go.solution-tree.com/instruction** to download this page.

6. You have a car shelter in your yard. Will your new SUV fit in it? Be sure to support your answer with calculations and reasoning.

Dimensions of the Shelter

Width: 224 cm
Length: 369 cm
Height: 190 cm

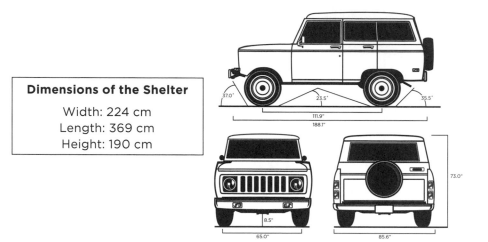

Source: Created by Julia Bilenkis. Adapted with permission.

Sample Kindergarten Report Card

(includes only learning/social behavior and language arts)

Name:	Kindergarten Report	Attendance	FALL	WINTER	SPRING
Teacher:		Half Days Absent	_____	_____	_____
School:		Times Tardy	_____	_____	_____

LEARNING/SOCIAL BEHAVIOR

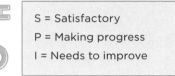

S = Satisfactory
P = Making progress
I = Needs to improve

We believe that these behaviors contribute to student learning and are considered an integral part of our teaching. We do not expect that all children will demonstrate consistency at all times, but we do emphasize continual progress for the student in demonstrating the behavior on a regular basis. Your child's progress is indicated according to the KEY to the left.

Demonstrates responsibility for own learning.

	Fall	Winter	Spring
1. Shows interest and is involved in learning.			
2. Attends to the task at hand.			
3. Completes tasks independently.			

Responds to teacher-directed activities.

	Fall	Winter	Spring
4. Listens attentively.			
5. Participates constructively in discussions.			
6. Participates constructively in activities.			
7. Follows directions.			

Demonstrates self-discipline.

	Fall	Winter	Spring
8. Follows rules.			
9. Demonstrates self control.			
10. Uses time wisely.			

Interacts positively with peers and adults.

	Fall	Winter	Spring
11. Respects the rights of others.			
12. Works cooperatively with others.			
13. Interacts positively with others.			
14. Solves problems constructively.			

Puts forth effort.

15. Perseveres even when tasks are difficult.			
16. Willing to take risks and try new things.			
17. Chooses and accepts tasks that challenge abilities.			

Page 1 of 3

WRITING

B = Beginning
D = Developing
S = Secure

The expectations for achievement are that students will meet Secure (S) proficiency levels by spring. The shaded area indicates when the outcome is usually first assessed.

Writing Genre			
F	**W**	**S**	**CONCEPTS/SKILLS**
▓			1. Writes a brief personal story using pictures, words, and/or sentences.
		▓	2. Reads and tries to copy different styles of poetry.
		▓	3. Writes a brief informational piece using drawings, words, and/or sentences as a page for a class book.
		▓	4. Helps with a class research project by adding key information gathered from materials supplied by the teacher.
Writing Process			
▓			5. Brainstorms ideas for narrative stories.
▓			6. Produces pictures and drawings that fit the story.
	▓		7. As s/he plans to write, with help from the teacher, thinks about how the readers will react.
▓			8. Spells words based on how they sound when writing.
		▓	9. Brainstorms ideas for informational text.
		▓	10. Makes changes to writing by reading it to a friend, and asks for ideas to improve it to make the meaning more clear.
Personal Style			
	▓		11. Expresses feelings, uses his/her natural language, and creates new ideas to show originality in his/her speech and writing.
Spelling			
	▓		12. Uses beginning and simple ending sounds, or word lists provided by the teacher to figure out how to spell more words.
		▓	13. Correctly spells about 18 words s/he sees often and finds meaningful.
Handwriting			
▓			14. Writes from left to right and top to bottom.
	▓		15. Forms upper- and lowercase letters.
		▓	16. Leaves spaces between words when writing.
Writing Attitude			
▓	▓	▓	17. Is eager to write and learn to write.

READING

Behaviors are dated (F= Fall, W= Winter, S= Spring) when they are seen routinely over time at a "secure" level. A behavior flagged as I= Needs Improvement.

Pre-K (Emergent Reader)	Kindergarten (Developing Reader)	Grade 1 (Beginning Reader)
Comprehension ____ Demonstrates comprehension of a story through comments, reactions, discussion, and/or drawing ____ Retells a familiar story, with beginning, middle, and end with book support **Strategies** ____ Holds book and turns pages correctly ____ Demonstrates left to right movement ____ Identifies 15–20 of 54 letter names ____ Recognizes familiar print such as names or signs **Listening and Speaking** ____ Communicates wants and needs verbally ____ Has vocabulary to name common objects and discuss everyday experiences	**Comprehension** ____ Reads books with predictable text (Level C) ____ Memorizes pattern books, poems, and familiar books ____ Retells a familiar story read to student with beginning, middle, and end without book support ____ Demonstrates personal connection to stories read or heard through comments, reactions, discussion, and/or drawing **Strategies** ____ Identifies 21–46 of 54 letter names ____ Identifies 47–54 of 54 letter names ____ Rhymes and plays with words ____ Uses information from pictures to construct meaning ____ Uses a sight word vocabulary of 10–15 words ____ Uses at least 20 sounds in reading/writing contexts ____ Uses 1:1 correspondence to track print ____ Uses print and illustrations to problem solve text **Listening and Speaking** ____ Gives detailed descriptions of needs, wants, and events ____ Listens to others without interrupting	**Comprehension** ____ Reads and comprehends books at Level I ____ Reads aloud with fluency and expression ____ Retells stories, read independently, to reflect sequence, setting, characters, problem, and resolution ____ Identifies main idea and supporting details of informational text read independently **Strategies** ____ Uses visual cues ____ Uses structure cues ____ Uses meaning cues ____ Self-corrects miscues that affect meaning ____ Uses multiple strategies automatically as needed to problem solve text **Listening and Speaking** ____ Responds to others using complete sentences ____ Uses questions and statements in appropriate contexts

Current Instructional Reading Level for this Report Card Period.

The Instructional Reading Level for each marking period is indicated below. The slide/bar graph provides a visual representation of progress.	Reading Targets by Grade		
	Kindergarten	**First Grade**	**Second Grade**
	Prior to June—Level A June—Level C	November—Level D March—Level G June—Level I	November—Level J March—Level L June—Level M

_____ Fall–November _____ Winter–March _____ Spring–June

Fall	Pre-Reader
Winter	
Spring	

Source: Kindergarten Learning Project (2008). Grateful acknowledgment to the Kindergarten Learning Project Team, the British Columbia Ministry of Education, and Qualicum British Columbia School District 69. Reprinted with permission.

Page 3 of 3

Short Story to Support Nanci's Differentiated English Lesson

The Story of an Hour

by Kate Chopin

Knowing that Mrs. Mallard was afflicted with a heart trouble, great care was taken to break to her as gently as possible the news of her husband's death.

It was her sister Josephine who told her, in broken sentences; veiled hints that revealed in half concealing. Her husband's friend Richards was there, too, near her. It was he who had been in the newspaper office when intelligence of the railroad disaster was received, with Brently Mallard's name leading the list of "killed." He had only taken the time to assure himself of its truth by a second telegram, and had hastened to forestall any less careful, less tender friend in bearing the sad message.

She did not hear the story as many women have heard the same, with a paralyzed inability to accept its significance. She wept at once, with sudden, wild abandonment, in her sister's arms. When the storm of grief had spent itself she went away to her room alone. She would have no one follow her.

There stood, facing the open window, a comfortable, roomy armchair. Into this she sank, pressed down by a physical exhaustion that haunted her body and seemed to reach into her soul.

She could see in the open square before her house the tops of trees that were all aquiver with the new spring life. The delicious breath of rain was in the air. In the street below a peddler was crying his wares. The notes of a distant song which someone was singing reached her faintly, and countless sparrows were twittering in the eaves.

There were patches of blue sky showing here and there through the clouds that had met and piled one above the other in the west facing her window.

She sat with her head thrown back upon the cushion of the chair, quite motionless, except when a sob came up into her throat and shook her, as a child who has cried itself to sleep continues to sob in its dreams.

She was young, with a fair, calm face, whose lines bespoke repression and even a certain strength. But now there was a dull stare in her eyes, whose gaze was fixed away off yonder on one of those patches of blue sky. It was not a glance of reflection, but rather indicated a suspension of intelligent thought.

Page 1 of 3

There was something coming to her and she was waiting for it, fearfully. What was it? She did not know; it was too subtle and elusive to name. But she felt it, creeping out of the sky, reaching toward her through the sounds, the scents, the color that filled the air.

Now her bosom rose and fell tumultuously. She was beginning to recognize this thing that was approaching to possess her, and she was striving to beat it back with her will—as powerless as her two white slender hands would have been.

When she abandoned herself a little whispered word escaped her slightly parted lips. She said it over and over under her breath: "free, free, free!" The vacant stare and the look of terror that had followed it went from her eyes.

They stayed keen and bright. Her pulses beat fast, and the coursing blood warmed and relaxed every inch of her body.

She did not stop to ask if it were or were not a monstrous joy that held her. A dear and exalted perception enabled her to dismiss the suggestion as trivial.

She knew that she would weep again when she saw the kind, tender hands folded in death; the face that had never looked save with love upon her, fixed and gray and dead. But she saw beyond that bitter moment a long procession of years to come that would belong to her absolutely. And she opened and spread her arms out to them in welcome.

There would be no one to live for her during those coming years; she would live for herself. There would be no powerful will bending hers in that blind persistence with which men and women believe they have a right to impose a private will upon a fellow-creature. A kind intention or a cruel intention made the act seem no kiss less a crime as she looked upon it in that brief moment of illumination.

And yet she had loved him—sometimes. Often she had not. What did it matter! What could love, the unsolved mystery, count for in face of this possession of self-assertion which she suddenly recognized as the strongest impulse of her being!

"Free! Body and soul free!" she kept whispering.

Josephine was kneeling before the closed door with her lips to the keyhole, imploring for admission. "Louise, open the door! I beg; open the door—you will make yourself ill. What are you doing, Louise? For heaven's sake open the door."

"Go away. I am not making myself ill." No; she was drinking in a very elixir of life through that open window.

Her fancy was running riot along those days ahead of her. Spring days, and summer days, and all sorts of days that would be her own. She breathed a quick prayer that life might be long. It was only yesterday she had thought with a shudder that life might be long.

She arose at length and opened the door to her sister's importunities. There was a feverish triumph in her eyes, and she carried herself unwittingly like a goddess of Victory. She clasped her sister's waist, and together they descended the stairs. Richards stood waiting for them at the bottom.

Someone was opening the front door with a latchkey. It was Brently Mallard who entered, a little travel-stained, composedly carrying his grip-sack and umbrella. He had been far from the scene of accident, and did not even know there had been one. He stood amazed at Josephine's piercing cry; at Richards' quick motion to screen him from the view of his wife.

But Richards was too late.

When the doctors came they said she had died of heart disease—of joy that kills.

Kate Chopin (1851–1904) was an American writer. The Story of an Hour *was published in 1894.*

Research Process Checklist

Name: _____ **Term:** _____

Record the date each time you use this checklist.
Make a check mark under the date when you are able to reply "Yes" to the question.

	Date											
Have I asked appropriate questions to guide my research?												
Have I considered a wide range of appropriate primary and/or secondary sources?												
Have I produced a workable research question?												
Have I revised my research question, as necessary, according to results of my research?												
Have I located a wide range of appropriate primary and/or secondary sources?												
Have I made appropriate selections of sources based on relevance to topic, reliability, and variety of perspectives/degree of bias?												
Have I recorded the information in a systematic way?												
Have I recorded the sources of all information?												
Have I classified or categorized the information appropriately and effectively?												
Have I created notes and graphic organizers to represent the information effectively?												
Have I synthesized and evaluated my findings with accuracy?												
Have I formulated a thesis statement that answers my research question?												
Have I identified sufficient supporting evidence to explain and defend my thesis?												
Summary of Things I Need to Work On												

From Cooper. Talk About Assessment HS Flyer *2009–10. © 2010 Nelson Education Ltd. Reproduced by permission. www.cengage.com/permissions*

Music Rubric for 11–14 Year Olds

KS3 Levels		Unit	Date	Sig.
	Sing in tune with expression.			
	Perform simple melodies or rhythms.			
	Improvise repeated patterns.			
	Combine layers of sound with awareness of the effect.			
	Recognize how the different musical elements are combined and used expressively.			
	Make improvements to my own work.			
Level 4				
	Perform from simple notations.			
	Maintain my own part with awareness of others.			
	Improvise melodies and rhythms.			
	Compose using musical shapes.			
	Describe, compare, and discuss different kinds of music using musical vocabulary.			
	Suggest improvements to my own work and others' work.			
Level 5				
	Perform parts from memory and notations, e.g., taking a solo part and/or providing rhythms.			
	Improvise melodies and rhythms within given structures.			
	Compose music for different occasions using a variety of notations.			
	Evaluate how venue, occasion, and purpose affect the way music is created, performed, and heard.			
	Refine and improve my work.			

Source: Walkden High School, Worsley, Manchester, United Kingdom.

REFERENCES AND RESOURCES

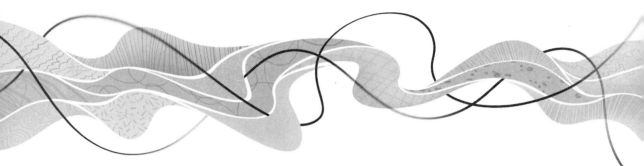

Ann Arbor Public Schools. (2009). *Kindergarten report.* Ann Arbor, MI: Author. Accessed at www.aaps.k12.mi.us/aaps.forparents/files/kindergarten.pdf on February 17, 2011.

Ault, K., Dawson, R., & MacCulloch, R. (2009). *Assessment begins in kindergarten.* Unpublished report, Upper Canada District School Board, Ontario, Canada.

Author. (2007). *Student success grade 7 & 8: Differentiated instruction educator's package.* Toronto, ON: Queen's Printer for Ontario.

Black, P., Harrison, C., Lee, C., Marshall, B., & Wiliam, D. (2003). *Assessment for learning: Putting it into practice.* Berkshire, England: Open University Press.

Black, P., Harrison, C., Lee, C., Marshall, B., & Wiliam, D. (2004). Working inside the black box: Assessment for learning in the classroom. *Phi Delta Kappan, 86*(1), 8.

Black, P., & Wiliam, D. (1998). *Inside the black box: Raising standards through classroom assessment.* London: King's College London School of Education. Accessed at http://weaeducation.typepad.co.uk/files/blackbox-1.pdf on February 17, 2011.

Chopin, K. (2001). *The story of an hour.* Logan, IA: Perfection Learning.

Cooper, D. (2006). *Talk about assessment: Strategies and tools to improve learning.* Scarborough, ON: Nelson Education.

Cooper, D. (2010). *Talk about assessment: High school strategies and tools.* Scarborough, ON: Nelson Education.

Cooper, D., & O'Connor, K. (2008). *Communicating student learning: Guidelines for schools—In consultation with Manitoba Education, Citizenship and Youth.* Winnipeg, MB: Government of Manitoba.

Csikszentmihalyi, M. (1990). *Flow: The psychology of optimal experience.* New York: Harper & Row.

DuFour, R., DuFour, R., Eaker, R., & Karhanek, G. (2010). *Raising the bar and closing the gap: Whatever it takes.* Bloomington, IN: Solution Tree Press.

Debold, E. (2002). Flow with soul: An interview with Dr. Mihaly Csikszentmihalyi. *EnlightenNext, 21.* Accessed at www.enlightennext.org/magazine/j21/csiksz .asp? on February 17, 2011.

Earl, L. M. (2004). *Assessment as learning: Using classroom assessment to maximize student learning.* Thousand Oaks, CA: Corwin Press.

Florida Department of Education. (2008). *Next generation Sunshine State standards.* Accessed at www.floridastandards.org/Standards/FLStandardSearch .aspx on February 18, 2011.

Foothills School Division. (2010). *Learner profile 2009–2010.* High River, AB: Author. Accessed at www.fsd38.ab.ca/uploads/documents/Learner_Profile _Sample_May_2010.pdf on February 18, 2011.

Fullan, M., Hill, P., & Crévola, C. (2006). *Breakthrough.* Thousand Oaks, CA: Corwin Press.

Gardner, H. (1983). *Frames of mind: The theory of multiple intelligences.* New York: Basic Books.

Gregg, L. A. (2007). Crossing the canyon: Helping students with special needs achieve proficiency. In D. Reeves (Ed.), *Ahead of the curve: The power of assessment to transform teaching and learning* (pp. 165–181). Bloomington, IN: Solution Tree Press.

Guskey, T. R. (2006). Making high school grades meaningful. *Phi Delta Kappan, 87*(9), 670–675.

Hume, K., & Ledgerwood, B. (2008). 8b: No limits, secrets. In K. Hume & B. Ledgerwood, *Nelson literacy 8* (pp. 35–37). Toronto, ON: Nelson Education.

Hunt, D. E. (1987). *Beginning with ourselves: In practice, theory, and human affairs.* Cambridge, MA: Brookline Books.

Instructivist Archives. (2005, March 27). Multiple intelligences [Blog post]. Accessed at http://instructivist-archives.blogspot.com/2005_03_01_archive .html on February 18, 2011.

Jackson, R. R. (2009). *Never work harder than your students and other principles of great teaching.* Alexandria, VA: Association for Supervision and Curriculum Development.

Kagan, S. (1994). *Cooperative learning.* San Clemente, CA: Kagan.

Klingensmith, B. (Ed.). (2000). *History—Social science content standards for California Public Schools: Kindergarten through grade twelve.* Sacramento: California Department of Education. Accessed at www.cde.ca.gov/be/st/ss /documents/histsocscistnd.pdf on February 18, 2011.

Leahy, S., Lyon, C., Thompson, M., & Wiliam, D. (2005). Classroom assessment: Minute by minute, day by day. *Educational Leadership, 63*(3), 18–24. Accessed at

www.state.nj.us/education/njpep//classroom/arts_assessment/worddocs
/ClassroomAssessClas.pdf on February 18, 2011.

Manitoba Education, Citizenship and Youth. (2008). *Communicating student
learning: Guidelines for schools.* Winnipeg, MB: Author.

Massachusetts Department of Education. (2003). *Massachusetts history and social
science curriculum framework.* Malden, MA: Author. Accessed at www.doe
.mass.edu/frameworks/hss/final.pdf on February 18, 2011.

McCarthy, B. (1996). *About learning.* Barrington, IL: Excel.

Montcrest School. (2006). *Interim report card.* Toronto, ON: Author.

Murrieta Valley Unified School District. (2007). *Academic standards trimester
report, 2007–2008.* Murrieta, CA: Author. Accessed at www.murrieta.k12
.ca.us/14881092415365630/site/default.asp on June 16, 2011.

Nelley, E., & Smith, A. (2001). *PM benchmarks reading assessment.* Scarborough,
ON: Nelson Education.

New Jersey Department of Education. (2009). *New Jersey core curriculum content
standards: New Jersey World Class standards.* Accessed at https://www13.state
.nj.us/NJCCCS/Worldclassstandards.aspx on April 18, 2011.

O'Connor, K. (2009). *How to grade for learning, K–12* (3rd ed.). Thousand Oaks, CA:
Corwin Press.

O'Connor, K. (2011). *A repair kit for grading: 15 fixes for broken grades* (2nd ed.).
Boston: Pearson.

Ontario Ministry of Education. (2006). *The Ontario curriculum, grades 1–8:
Language, 2006* (Rev. ed.). Toronto, ON: Queen's Printer for Ontario. Accessed
at www.edu.gov.on.ca/eng/document/curricul/curricul.html on December 16,
2010.

Ontario Ministry of Education. (2007a). *The Ontario curriculum, grades 9 and 10:
English, 2007* (Rev. ed.). Toronto, ON: Queen's Printer for Ontario. Accessed at
www.edu.gov.on.ca/eng/curriculum/secondary/english.html on February 18,
2011.

Ontario Ministry of Education. (2007b). *The Ontario curriculum, grades 1–8: Science and technology, 2007.* Toronto, ON: Queen's Printer for Ontario. Accessed at
www.edu.gov.on.ca/eng/curriculum/elementary/scientec.html on February 18,
2011.

Ontario Ministry of Education. (2010). *Growing success: Assessment, evaluation,
and reporting in Ontario schools.* Toronto, ON: Queen's Printer for Ontario.

Ontario Ministry of Education. (2010). *Overall expectations (from The Ontario
Curriculum, grades 9 and 10: English [Rev. ed.]).* Toronto, ON: Queen's Printer for
Ontario.

Partnership for 21st Century Skills. (2006). *Framework for 21st century learning.* Accessed at www.p21.org/index.php?option=com_content&task=view&id=266&Itemid=120 on February 18, 2011.

Pearson, D., & Gallagher, M. C. (1983). The instruction of reading comprehension. *Contemporary Educational Psychology, 8*(3), 317–344.

Prensky, M. (2001). Digital natives, digital immigrants. *On the Horizon, 9*(5), 1–6. Accessed at www.marcprensky.com/writing/Prensky%20-%20Digital%20Natives,%20Digital%20Immigrants%20-%20Part1.pdf on February 18, 2011.

Qualicum School District 69 Kindergarten Assessment Committee. (2008). *Kindergarten learning project.* Accessed at www.sd69.bc.ca/Programs-Services/ProfessionalNetworks/Pages/KLP.aspx on February 1, 2011.

Qualifications and Curriculum Development Agency. (1999). *National curriculum: Secondary curriculum—Music, key stage 3 & key stage 4.* Coventry, England: Author. Accessed at http://curriculum.qcda.gov.uk/key-stages-3-and-4/subjects/key-stage-3/music/Level-descriptions/index.aspx on October 8, 2010.

Reeves, D. B. (2004). The case against the zero. *Phi Delta Kappan, 86*(4), 324–325.

Reeves, D. B. (2007). From the bell curve to the mountain: A new vision for achievement, assessment, and equity. In D. B. Reeves (Ed.), *Ahead of the curve: The power of assessment to transform teaching and learning* (pp. 1–10). Bloomington, IN: Solution Tree Press.

Spandel, V. (2002). *Write traits.* Wilmington, MA: Great Source Education Group.

Sternberg, R. J. (1985). *Beyond IQ: A triarchic theory of human intelligence.* New York: Cambridge University Press.

Stiggins, R. J., Arter, J. A., Chappuis, J., & Chappuis, S. (2004). *Classroom assessment for student learning: Doing it right—using it well.* Portland, OR: Assessment Training Institute.

Strickland, C. A. (2007). *Tools for high-quality differentiated instruction: An ASCD action tool.* Alexandria, VA: Association for Supervision and Curriculum Development.

Subotnik, R., & Cogan, J. (2004). *The other 3 Rs: Reasoning, resilience, and responsibility—A 2-year pilot study funded by the James S. McDonnell Foundation.* Washington, DC: American Psychological Association. Accessed at www.apa.org/ed/schools/cpse/publications/3rs-defined.aspx# on February 18, 2011.

Sullivan Palincsar, A., & Brown, A. L. (1984). Reciprocal teaching of comprehension-fostering and comprehension-monitoring activities. *Cognition and Instruction, 1*(2), 117–175. Accessed at http://people.ucsc.edu/~gwells/Files/Courses_Folder/ED%20261%20Papers/Palincsar%20Reciprocal%20Teaching.pdf on February 18, 2011.

Tomlinson, C. A. (1999). *The differentiated classroom: Responding to the needs of all learners.* Alexandria, VA: Association for Supervision and Curriculum Development.

Tomlinson, C. A. (2001). *How to differentiate instruction in mixed-ability classrooms* (2nd ed.). Alexandria, VA: Association for Supervision and Curriculum Development.

Tomlinson, C. A., & McTighe, J. (2006). *Integrating differentiated instruction and understanding by design: Connecting content and kids.* Alexandria, VA: Association for Supervision and Curriculum Development.

Traub, J. (1998, October 26). Multiple intelligence disorder: Howard Gardner's campaign against logic. *The New Republic.* Accessed at http://instructivist-archives.blogspot.com/2005_03_01_archive.html on December 16, 2010.

Ungerleider, C. (2008). *Evaluation of the Ontario Ministry of Education's Student Success/Learning to 18 Strategy: Final report.* Ottawa, ON: Canadian Council on Learning. Accessed at www.edu.gov.on.ca/eng/teachers/studentsuccess/CCL_SSE_Report.pdf on February 18, 2011.

Vygotsky, L. S. (1978). Interaction between learning and development. In M. Cole (Ed.), *Mind in society: The development of higher psychological processes* (pp. 84–91). Cambridge, MA: Harvard University Press.

Wente, M. (2009, April 18). We pretend to teach 'em, they pretend to learn. *The Globe and Mail,* p. A23.

Wiggins, G. (1994a). *Standards, not standardization: A video and print curriculum on performance-based student assessment.* Alexandria, VA: Association for Supervision and Curriculum Development.

Wiggins, G. (1994b). Toward better report cards. *Educational Leadership, 52*(2), 28–37. Accessed at www.ascd.org/publications/educational-leadership/oct94/vo152/numo2/Toward-Better-Report-Cards.aspx on February 18, 2011.

Wiggins, G., & McTighe, J. (1998). *Understanding by design.* Alexandria, VA: Association for Supervision and Curriculum Development.

Wiliam, D. (2001). What is wrong with our educational assessments and what can be done about it. *Education Review, 15*(1), 57–62. Accessed at http://search.conduit.com/Results.aspx?q=wiliam%2C+dylan%2C+goodhart%27s+law&meta=all&hl=en&gl=ca&SelfSearch=1&SearchSourceOrigin=10&ctid=CT2405723&octid=CT2405723 on December 16, 2010.

Wormeli, R. (2006). *Fair isn't always equal: Assessing and grading in the differentiated classroom.* Portland, ME: Stenhouse.

INDEX

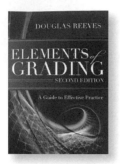

Elements of Grading: A Guide to Effective Practice (Second Edition)
Douglas Reeves
Learn how to define proficiency accurately and differentiate to help all students achieve it. Using stories, strategies, case histories, and sample documents, the author explains how to implement equitable instruction, assessment, grading, and reporting practices for diverse 21st century learners. **BKF412**

Differentiation and the Brain: How Neuroscience Supports the Learner-Friendly Classroom
David A. Sousa and Carol Ann Tomlinson
Examine the basic principles of differentiation in light of educational neuroscience research that will help you make the most effective curricular, instructional, and assessment choices. Learn how to implement differentiation so that it achieves the desired result of shared responsibility between teacher and student. **BKF353**

Defensible Differentiation: What Does It Take to Get It Right?
Carol Ann Tomlinson
One-size-fits-all instruction approaches do not serve today's academically diverse student population, and simply claiming to practice differentiation is not a magic bullet. In this keynote, Carol Ann Tomlinson calls on teachers to implement differentiation best practices to serve today's academically diverse student population. **DVF053**

Supporting Differentiated Instruction: A Professional Learning Communities Approach
Robin J. Fogarty and Brian M. Pete
Foreword by Jay McTighe
Examine how PLCs provide the decision-making platform for the rigorous work of differentiated classroom instruction. A practical guide to implementing differentiation in the classroom, this book offers a roadmap to effective teaching that responds to diverse learning needs. **BKF348**

Solution Tree | Press

a division of
Solution Tree

Visit solution-tree.com or call 800.733.6786 to order.